Praise for TRACEY DILS'S *YOU CAN WRITE CHILDREN'S BOOKS*

"Extremely helpful to emerging children's book writers. All of the best tools are here! *You Can Write Children's Books* gives writers the encouragement, guidance and inside information needed to be successful in today's children's book market. New authors will be published because of this insightful book."

—Tanya Dean, vice-president, Pages Publishing Group

"From her vantage point as a published writer and experienced editor, Tracey Dils takes the mystery out of the maze of children's book publishing. Her *You Can Write Children's Books* is a how-to text packed with professional know-how and the inside information that can turn wannabe scribblers into effective writers, and help them sell their work."

—Oscar Collier, literary agent and author (with Frances Spatz Leighton) of *How to Write and Sell Your First Novel* and *How to Write and Sell Your First Nonfiction Book*

"Tracey Dils's book is practical, helpful, accessible and delightful to read. It's a how-to book for anyone interested in writing for children. But—it goes further—it's a why book, prodding readers to think deeply about their reasons for wanting to write for children. A course in itself—I highly recommend it!"

—Mimi Chenfeld, educator and author of *Creative Experiences for Young Children* and *Teaching Language Arts Creatively*

"Bravo to Tracey for such a comprehensive look at writing for kids, from the very young to the middle grade reader! I wish I'd had this book when I was starting out!"

—Lurlene McDaniel, young adult novelist, Bantam Books

You Can Write Children's Books

TRACEY E. DILS

WRITER'S DIGEST BOOKS
CINCINNATI, OHIO

 Published by Writer's Digest Books, an imprint of F&W Publications, Inc., 1507 Dana Avenue, Cincinnati, Ohio 45207. (800) 289-0963. First edition.

Other fine Writer's Digest Books are available from your local bookstore or direct from the publisher.

Visit our Web site at www.writersdigest.com for information on more resources for writers.

To receive a free biweekly E-mail newsletter delivering tips and updates about writing and about Writer's Digest products, send an E-mail with "Subscribe Newsletter" in the body of the message to newsletter-request@writersdigest.com or register directly at our Web site at www.writersdigest.com.

02 01 6 5 4

Library of Congress Cataloging-in-Publication Data

Dils, Tracey E.
You can write children's books / by Tracey E. Dils.—1st ed.
p. cm.
Includes bibliographical references and index.
ISBN 0-89879-829-9 (alk. paper)
1. Children's literature—Authorship. 2. Children's literature—Marketing.
I. Title.
PN147.5.D55 1998
808.06′8—dc21 97-47235
CIP

Edited by Jack Heffron and Alice Buening
Production edited by Michelle Howry
Interior design by Sandy Kent
Cover design by Brian Roeth

DEDICATION

To Richard, Emily and Phillip
Thank you for giving me support, love and balance.

With special thanks to
Patricia Houston, Lisa Harkrader, Jennifer Westfall and Kate Kenah for their assistance in preparing this manuscript.

About the Author

Tracey E. Dils is the award-winning author of more than twenty books for young readers in a variety of genres—picture books, scary stories, beginning readers, nonfiction science titles and a biography. She has held a number of high-level editorial positions, including marketing manager for The Ohio State University Press and editor-in-chief at Willowisp Press. Currently, Dils is assistant fiction editor for *Guideposts for Kids* magazine and acts as a freelance editor for several children's publishing houses and packagers.

Dils considers inspiring beginning writers to be some of her most important work. She has taught writing for children at the university level and through correspondence schools, and she is a featured speaker at writers' conferences and workshops throughout the country. In addition to her work with aspiring adult writers, Dils has taught writing to children in a variety of settings, and is a frequent "guest author" in elementary and middle schools.

Tracey Dils lives in Columbus, Ohio, with her husband Richard Herrold and their two children, Emily and Phillip.

TABLE OF CONTENTS

1 WHAT YOU NEED TO KNOW TO GET STARTED

To touch the lives of children.

That was what I wanted to do when I set out to write children's books some fifteen years ago.

Of course, I had other goals too. I knew that writing children's books looked like great fun. The books I remembered from my own childhood and the ones I was reading to my own children were full of whimsy, magic, fantasy and outrageous humor. The books I loved used language in wildly creative ways, invented incredible worlds and developed wonderful—sometimes crazy—characters and plots. The whole idea sounded like, well, child's play. I couldn't wait to take my computer and head to that playground of children's books.

But in my heart, I wanted to write books that would inspire and touch children. And to do that, I knew that I couldn't just write them—I had to get them published.

And that's where I came to a standstill. I didn't know how to go about doing that.

That may be where you are, too. You may have some wonderful ideas about children's stories, and you may even have some terrific stories written. But, like me, you've heard the tales of harried editors, their desks stacked with huge piles of manuscripts from hopeful authors. You've heard about how competitive the entire field of publishing is. And you've heard about those horrible rejection letters.

It *is* true that it's not easy to publish children's books. But the more you learn about the field and the business of children's publishing, the better equipped you will be to achieve success. That's what this book is about—giving you the information and advice you need to confidently enter the field and publish your work, so that ultimately, you can touch the lives of children.

Misconceptions About Writing for Children

Let's start with what you *think* you know about children's book publishing. Most writers who are considering writing children's books have some preconceived notions about the genre. Many of these ideas are probably right on. Others are misconceptions that we'll want to clear up before we go any further.

1. Writing children's books is easier than writing for the adult market because the books are shorter. Because of the special nature of this audience and the competitive nature of the market, most writers find that writing for children is as challenging or *more* challenging than writing for other audiences.

2. Stories for children need to teach a moral lesson. While many of the stories we remember from childhood preached lessons about right and wrong, today's publishers are looking for stories that suggest hopeful messages subtly or that simply depict a "slice of life." Moreover, young readers are turned off by heavy-handed morals. They can figure out a story's implications for themselves, without having the morals spelled out for them.

3. Because my kids love the stories that I tell them at bedtime, I'm sure they are good enough to be published. While your own kids—and even their friends—probably love your stories, this small sample of children is probably not an indication of the market as a whole.

4. I have a great idea for a picture book, but I don't know how to find an illustrator. This is probably the biggest misconception about writing picture books. Publishers—not authors—almost always find and work with the illustrators of the books they publish. In fact, most publishing companies prefer to work this way.

5. Kids can think abstractly. While some young readers can think abstractly, most children (especially younger children) understand fiction quite literally. That means you have to be careful about what you suggest to them. Perhaps you have a story idea about a little girl who is lonely. Suddenly, a magical man arrives and takes her away on a fantastic adventure. That may be a solid story idea, but your reader might also take that story line literally, and the repercussions of that in today's world could be very dangerous.

6. Kids are fairly unsophisticated consumers. Today's kids are selective consumers—of everything from athletic shoes to their own books. Do not underestimate this sophistication.

7. You need an agent to publish children's books. As competitive as today's market is, many children's book editors are still reading unsolicited material and delight in finding a gem of a story in their "slush pile."

8. If I send my story out to a publisher, they might just steal my idea! Publishers are simply not going to steal your idea. Chances are, your idea isn't entirely original anyway. The old adage, "there's nothing new under the sun" applies here. There's not an idea for a book that hasn't been invented before.

9. I need to protect my work with a copyright before I send it out. Your work is protected by federal copyright laws whether or not you apply for a copyright through the U.S. copyright office. Don't place a © notice on the manuscript—the work is protected without it. By using one, you'll only end up looking naive to a publisher. If you are still concerned, you can ensure that your work will be protected in a court of law by mailing a copy of it to yourself in a self-addressed stamped envelope. When the envelope arrives at your mailbox, don't open it. Keep it sealed in a file. The post-mark will help you defend the work if you need to.

The Business of Children's Book Publishing

You may find it difficult to think of children's book publishing as a big business, but that's exactly what it is. Indeed, when you are pondering a book idea that is dear to your heart, it can overwhelm your creative sensibilities to even begin to consider what a big business it is. Still, knowing a little bit about how children's book

Is Writing for Children for You?

Can you answer yes to all of the questions below?

- Do you enjoy spending time with children? Do you truly *like* children?
- Do you aspire to a loftier goal than just "being published"?
- Do you consider writing for children an admirable pursuit, or have you chosen this field because you think it's somehow easier than writing for "grown-ups"?
- Do you truly love *reading* books written for young readers? Do you frequently choose to read children's books instead of books written for "grown-ups"?
- Are you willing to work hard, not only on your writing, but on researching and getting to know the market?
- Are you open to exploring the wide variety of literature available for children?
- Have you thought about the role good books play in a child's life?

publishing has evolved will help you to shape your own children's books.

Until the late sixties, children's book publishing was a relatively small part of the overall publishing business. Publishers published only a few new children's books a year and relied on a small number of well-known authors—like Dr. Seuss, E.B. White and Robert McClosky.

All that has changed. Children's publishing grew up in the 1970s, and this growth turned a small and cozy corner of the book world into a billion-dollar business.

The growth process was a difficult one. Publishing companies merged with each other. Editors moved from publishing house to publishing house, often taking their authors with them. For a period in the late eighties and early nineties, the world of children's book publishing seemed like total chaos.

Then things settled down. While there is still some "editor hopping" and there are still plenty of mergers and acquisitions, the industry seems to be getting its act together in terms of the business side of children's publishing. The result: Children's publishers have

How to Keep Up

• **Read popular children's magazines.** You can find a nice selection at your library or bookstore. Because most magazines are monthly, they can respond to trends much quicker than book publishers. You can often get a sense of what the next trend in children's book publishing is going to be by studying kid's magazines.

• **Read publishing and library trade magazines.** I strongly recommend *Publishers Weekly* (*PW*), which is the bible of the publishing industry and an excellent reference. Each issue contains reviews, information about the publishing industry and news about editorial appointments. Twice a year, *PW* publishes a children's announcement issue. These contain not only announcements for forthcoming children's books, but also advertisements, reviews, interviews and market industry figures. (The annoucement issue can be bought separately even if you don't have a subscription, and the cost is well worth the information provided.) Other trade publications I recommend include:

American Bookseller
Booklist
Book Report
Children's Literature Review
Five Owls
Horn Book
Kidscreen
School Library Journal
The Web

• **Read the newspaper.** Keep a file of newspaper or other articles that apply to children, the business of marketing to children, new theories of development, your specific subject matter, etc.

• **Talk to librarians and teachers.** Keep in touch with those people in your community who are closest to your target audience and to books. Pick their brains about what kids are into these days, what they are reading and what the latest trends are.

• **Spend time with your target audience.** Be deliberate about spending time with kids—and not just your own children. Volunteer at a school library, get involved with a church youth group or figure out another way to get firsthand experience with kids. The best way to learn to write for kids is to get to know them—and this means spending time doing just that.

- **Attend writers' conferences.** Many organizations and colleges sponsor writers' conferences. The Society for Children's Book Writers and Illustators, the large national organization for those who write and illustrate children's books, sponsors regional conferences and one large comprehensive conference in the summer.
- **Be aware of trends in other media areas.** Keep informed about television programs, musical groups and movies that are popular among the readers you are writing for. Those trends can suggest book ideas or tie-ins, as well as give you a sense of what today's kids like.
- **Be cognizant of demographic trends.** Recent statistics indicate that there will be a peak in the current baby boom in the year 2006. The number of Hispanic Americans between the ages of five and seventeen is expected to increase by 2.5 million and African Americans by one million. Most of the growth will occur in the suburbs, especially in the Southeast and the West. These statistics should suggest something to writers about what kinds of characters they should be creating and which age groups publishers will be targeting.

learned how to publish books that make them more of a profit.

For writers, this means there are many more opportunities to get published since there are simply more books being produced. And there are more creative opportunities, too. Publishers are trying new formats and new book/product combinations, and they are taking chances on innovative and creative topics and projects. Children's book authors are getting better financial deals and stronger publicity support.

And as the children's book publishing business has grown, it has been affected by the same forces that affect adult publishing. One of the most powerful of these forces is the trend toward diversity. It's easy to see how the world of children's publishing is responding to the improved awareness of our country's diversity. Publishers are creating more and more books with ethnic characters and focusing on other multicultural themes, including folk tales.

The influence of population trends isn't as easy to see, unless you know a bit about how these trends work. To illustrate these trends, demographers frequently refer to the image of a "pig in the python." Imagine a python as it swallows a pig. Think about how

Children's Book Publishing: You Know More Than You Think

You don't have to overwhelm yourself with research to get ideas for books or acquire knowledge of the market. You can extrapolate much from your own knowledge base. Here are some ways to do so:

- **Track trends in television and other media.** Those of us who are writers shudder to think of studying television as a way to help our writing. But realistically, we realize that television is one of our competitors. Learning as much as we can about the competition is one way to beat it! Next time you sit down in front of a situation comedy, especially one with child characters specifically geared to the kid market, think about these issues and how you might apply them to your writing:

  What is the subject matter of the show?

  How is the conflict introduced?

  How does the show present cliffhangers before commercial breaks?

  What ages are the characters? How old are the siblings? What kinds of conflicts occur?

  What is the overall setting? How many times and at which points in the plot is there a scene change?

  How does the show "wrap up" its plot? Has the main character grown or changed as a result of what has happened?

- **Watch trends filter down.** Trends and fads that are popular at the college level will frequently filter down in some form to younger kids. Rollerblading and tie-dye T-shirts are just two examples. In the book world, the horror trend eventually filtered down to younger kids. If you watch what is going on with young adults, you can predict what might soon be popular with younger children.
- **Observe that kids read "up."** Kids like to read about characters who are just a little bit older than they are, especially when they reach the middle grade years—fourth grade and up.
- **Be conscious of buying behavior.** Just as kids have more control over the purchases they make as they grow older, they also make more independent decisions about the books they read. Preschoolers may have no real choices. First and second graders have a bit more autonomy. Those readers in the upper grades make even more independent decisions about what they buy, although their peers also can be an influential factor. ✷

the pig's mass moves through the python's body. That protrusion is very similar to bulges in the population caused by the baby boom generation and its children. These bulges represent the largest target audiences, and as the bulges move—or, as a group, become older—the target audience for books and other products changes with them. The success of the Goosebumps series, for instance, can partly be attributed to the bulge in the population of readers in middle grades at the time the series was released.

Making Sense of It All

This may seem overwhelming, especially if your goal is simply to write inspiring books that will touch, move and delight young readers, but it's not as complicated as it seems. First, you need to learn the categories of children's book publishing and the requirements of each category. The next three chapters will cover these topics.

After learning more about the field of children's book publishing, you must decide where you fit into it. The best way to weave your way through this complex and changing field is to arm yourself with information. As you consider all of the various nuances, restrictions and unwritten rules, take some time to consider the real value of what you are doing.

Think about yourself and your goals as a writer.

Then think about yourself and your goals as a writer for children.

The best way to become successful at it is to be true to your goals as a writer and your feelings about writing for this very special audience—the children who will become our future.

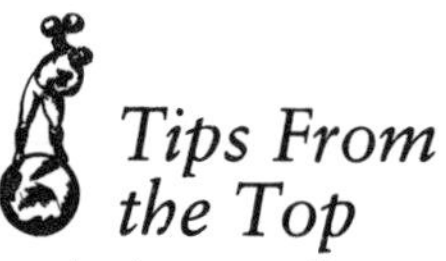

Tips From the Top

1. As you discover children's books that you like or enjoy sharing with your own children, take note of the publisher. Jot down favorite books and publisher information for future reference. These might be publishers you will want to approach with one of your manuscripts.

2. Spend as much time as you can with the audience that you anticipate writing for. Find ways to critically observe children (not your own) in various settings where they feel natural and comfortable

(e.g., bookstores, libraries, malls and parks). Take notes on what you observe.

3. Set up a writing space where you will enter your "writing mode." Think about the various things you might have in that space to inspire you. Begin gathering the tools you will need—pens and pencils, a computer, typewriter, dictionary, thesaurus, etc.

4. There are people in every community with a passion for children's literature. Find out who they are and strike up a professional friendship, if appropriate. These people may be writers, librarians, children's bookstore owners, teachers or parents.

5. Read children's books for all age categories—from picture books to those written for young adults. Explore contemporary titles as well as traditional favorites. Read books written for specific audiences—like the religious market—and general readership books.

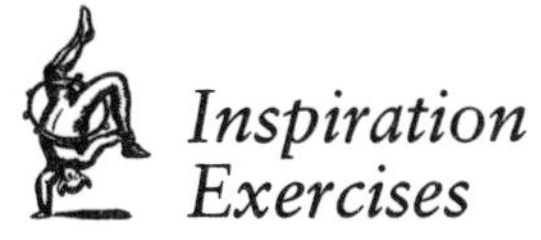

Inspiration Exercises

1. Choose a favorite book from your childhood. Reread it and jot down what you think about the book now and what you *think* you thought about it when you first read it.

2. Select a book from your local library that was published in the 1930s or 40s—*Mr. Popper's Penguins*, for example—and one written today. Think about how the two books differ in style, characters, plot and setting.

3. Consider your own life history. Are there experiences that might be the basis for a book? Are there experiences in the lives of the children you know? Begin jotting these down for future reference.

4. Glance through your newspaper and identify one or two articles about children. Try to imagine the details about those children—their daily lives, their personalities. Do the same with an article about a specific child. Make notes about your thoughts—notes about characters, situations or circumstances that might be good inspiration for future stories.

2 PICTURE BOOKS

To say that most writers who want to write for children want to write picture books is only a slight overgeneralization. Most of us think of picture books when we think of children's books. We remember the joy we discovered in the picture books we read as kids–even if they were as basic as the Curious George series, *Mike Mulligan and His Steam Shovel*, or *Good Night Moon*. Picture books unleashed our imaginations. They were the books that comforted us, that put us to sleep, that we shared on a lap with our loved ones.

For the same reasons, we continue to share picture books with our own children. Many adults read picture books with their kids long after their kids have gone on to reading chapter books. And there are many adults who choose picture books for their own leisure reading. There's a simple joy in opening a book that is both beautifully illustrated and beautifully written. The harmony between the written and the visual is where the magic of children's literature really happens.

But as simple as it is to enjoy a wonderful picture book, it is deceptively difficult to write one. Add to that the fact that there are literally thousands of writers submitting picture book manuscripts to publishers, and the task seems daunting.

Picture books are unlike any other genre. Arming yourself with basic knowledge about the form and style of picture books is necessary preparation for entering this overcrowded field. Then you must carefully consider the market and audience for your particular idea, and that is just the beginning. This chapter covers all the important details, from plotting to page count, as they apply to picture books.

The Market and the Audience

You may think that the market and the audience for a picture book are the same. But while kids preschool age through about second grade are your primary audience, they are not the real market.

Most kids do not buy picture books themselves; it is usually an adult who makes the purchase. The adult may be a librarian who shares books during story hour. It may be a teacher who is using a book in the classroom. It may be a grandparent who takes pride in selecting that one special book for a holiday or birthday gift. But most likely, it is a parent who is choosing the books his or her child will read.

What does this mean to you as a writer? You need to know that adults are your real market. For that reason, your story needs to be understood on at least two levels: It should appeal to an adult's sensibility and emotions, as well as to a child's very literal understanding of the basic story.

Adults may choose a particular picture book for their child for any number of reasons. It may be artistically, philosophically or nostagically appealing. Often adults select certain books because they see a redeeming value in the story. That doesn't mean the story needs to have a strong moral theme or that it must be educational in some way. It *does* mean that a picture book story needs to have a theme that both a grown-up and a child can relate to. Instilling a story with that redeeming value without hitting the reader over the head with a moral is one of the challenges of creating an appealing and marketable picture book.

Form and Length

Picture books cover a wide range of topics and subjects, are written in both verse and prose, and can be illustrated with a wide variety of media. They can even be completely wordless, the story told completely through the pictures.

But there is one thing that all picture books have in common. They all have a very structured format. In fact, picture books are probably the most structured category of children's books.

Simply stated, picture books have very specific page requirements. Because of the way the printing and binding process works, almost all picture books are either 24 or 32 pages long. The few exceptions that run longer or shorter all have a page count that is a multiple of eight. (The pages of all books are multiples of eight, but because picture books are by definition shorter, this specific page requirement is all the more important.) If you are just entering the field of children's writing, this restriction may come as a surprise to you. But it's an essential fact that must guide your writing.

Here's how the page count might affect your work. First, let's consider an average picture book of 32 pages. As a writer, you need to assume that some of those pages will contain what the publisher calls "front matter." These front matter pages, which generally do not have page numbers on them, include the title page, the copyright page, the dedication (although these two pages may be one and the same), and any additional "information pages" (information about a series of books, for example) that the publisher may choose to include.

That means your story—the actual *meat* of the picture book—will end up being only 28 published pages long.

The word count of your story, of course, can vary, but it probably should not exceed 2,000 words or so. And, if your story concept requires elaborate illustration, you'll need to adjust your word count accordingly.

Because of the restrictions on page count, the pacing of your story is extremely important. Most picture book writers find it helpful to actually "page" their book—they decide what words go on which pages. That way, they are certain their story will fit on the prescribed page count, and they have a sense of how their story will build and flow once it actually becomes a book. Of course, the final decision about pagination is up to the editor, but by paging your story, you will have insured that your book is long enough, detailed enough and exciting enough to fit the picture book category.

One way to page a book is to break the story into pages as you are writing, indicating page breaks as you type the story. A better way is to actually make a dummy picture book—a sample book in which you actually place the text on the appropriate page, allowing for the front matter pages. This way you'll be able to see how your story evolves through page spreads (two pages facing each other), and you'll learn something about the success of your story's pacing. You'll probably even revise your story a few more times based on what you have learned in the dummy process. (For instructions on making a picture book dummy, see pages 14-15.)

Should you send your dummy or your "paged" manuscript to an editor? The answer is no, unless the pagination is essential to the story itself, as it might be in a riddle book when the reader needs to turn a page to discover the answer. (We'll be discussing more about manuscript form in chapter seven).

You definitely *don't* want to send crude illustrations or even typed illustration suggestions along with a picture book proposal. (If the illustrations are essential to understanding the story, you might add a brief illustration note, but most editors can make sense of picture book manuscripts without illustration cues.)

While you may have some artistic talent, do not submit your art with the manuscript. Even if you know someone with experience, resist the temptation of asking him or her to illustrate your picture book before you send it out. Most editors like to make the marriage between illustrator and author themselves. While a few houses do accept book "packages" from author-illustrators or author/illustrator collaborations, most do not. Remember that an illustrator and an artist are not necessarily the same thing. The medium, the reproduction process and the technique are quite different. Even if your friend is a professional artist, he or she doesn't necessarily have what it takes to be a picture book illustrator.

Types of Picture Books

Unlike the other categories of books that we will explore later, there are not clear-cut kinds of picture books. The basic types of

How to Make a Picture Book Dummy

If you think that your picture book will run around thirty-two pages, take eight pages of typing paper and fold them in half so that they look like a book. You may staple them to hold them together if you like.

You now have a blank book of thirty-two pages. You may want to make several of these to allow for the variations which are explained below.

Decide whether your story would best start on a right-hand page (meaning the reader will read the material on the right-hand page, and then flip the page to the next spread) or whether it would better start on an actual two-page spread. While starting on the right-hand side gives you an extra page for your story, a spread can entice the reader with two pages of art.

If you've decided to begin your book on the right-hand page, write the words *title page* on the front of the dummy. On the next page (the first left-hand page), write *copyright/dedication*. Then take a typed version of your story and cut it into sections where you think the page breaks will occur.

Next, begin positioning your story throughout the rest of the pages. Remember to think about the pacing, the visual rhythm of the story and the overall length. Play around with positioning the story until you feel you have it right. You may need to cut up another copy of your story and start again. You may also decide to stop before going any further and revise your story.

If you've decided to begin your book on a two-page spread (the story will begin on the left-hand page), write the words *title page* on the first page of your dummy, *copyright* on the second page and *dedication* on the third. Then follow the same pattern as above, positioning the typed version of your story throughout as it feels appropriate.

After you've done this a few times, you may have changed your mind about whether you want your story to start on a right-hand page or a spread. Go back and rework it if you need to. You may also have discovered that your story is actually closer to twenty-four pages, rather than thirty-two. If that is the case, then remake a dummy with six pages of typing paper instead of eight. If necessary you can leave the last page of your book blank.

When you are finished with your dummy, review it thinking about these considerations:

- Is there enough action to illustrate on the spread you've chosen?
- Is there too much action to illustrate? (With some exceptions, you'll want to introduce one basic action or image per page or two-page spread.)
- Is there a variety of scenes or a variety of different actions of interest throughout the book?
- Does every page move the story forward, both in terms of the plot and in terms of the visual action?
- Will your story flow well with the art you envision?
- Are you writing a story or just writing captions?

Once you feel you have the dummy just right, go back to your story and indicate which words will go on which pages like this:

Page one: Title page

Page two: Copyright/dedication page

Page three: Once upon a time there was a very lonely bunny.

And so on.

books I suggest here are not meant to be prescriptive. There are picture books that don't fall into any of these categories, and, at the same time, there are picture books that fall into two or more. That said, editors tend to think about picture books in three general categories.

• **Story books** are by far the most popular kind of picture book. Story books are always fiction. They may also be retellings of folk or fairy tales. Usually, a story book involves a series of events leading to a climax and then a resolution. The resolution involves some sort of character growth on the part of the main character. In other words, as the character encounters the events of the story, he is somehow changed. He may have overcome a fear or learned something new about himself as he struggled with the conflict.

While it is too simple to think of story books as having a specific formula, many do follow a typical pattern. This pattern involves a main character who wants to achieve or acquire something. Three episodes of conflict follow, each one rising in intensity. During the final episode, the character strives the hardest to reach his goal and succeeds. The plot then resolves quickly.

- **Concept books** promote a child's understanding of his or her world. There are different kinds of concept books. They can actually teach an educational concept—like counting or telling time. Or, they can offer suggestions for overcoming one of childhood's many problems such as giving up a blanket, moving to a new house, starting school, etc. Concept books can be either fiction or nonfiction.
- **Novelty books**, which can also be fiction or nonfiction, rely on some sort of gimmick to tell the book's story. Pop-up books, seek-and-find books, and lift-the-flap books are all novelty books. Some titles, like the *Jolly Postman* by Allan and Janet Ahlberg, rely on a number of different novelties to engage the reader. The best novelty books incorporate the novelty into the book's story line. Eric Carle's *The Very Hungry Caterpillar*, for example, integrates the story line with several novelties, including graduated page lengths.

Subject Matter

The picture book genre accommodates a tremendous variety of subject matter, possibly more than any other category of children's books. However, there are certain conventions to consider when choosing subjects.

What picture book subjects are likely to strike an editor's fancy? The most common subjects for picture books are kids themselves. There are notable exceptions in which the story is about an adult, several adults, or an adult and a special pet, for instance. But for the most part, picture books are about kids and their dilemmas, problems and issues. Adults often play an important role in the plot, but it is the child character who needs to solve the story's problem.

It is often very difficult for well-meaning writers—since they are adults—to remove that adult perspective from a story. Too often, an adult voice intrudes or an adult character steps in to save the day and offer a solution to the story's problem. Picture books run into trouble, too, when they get bogged down in adult language or dialogue. I often tell beginning writers who are struggling with a plot to get rid of the grown-ups entirely. Write the story completely about children, then go back and add the grown-ups where needed.

It's not enough to rely on a child-centered conflict and child characters as your primary subject matter though. If you are writing a picture book, you'll also want your readers to see glimpses of the familiar "things" in their own lives on the pages of that book. These glimpses may be references to school routines, meals, daily rituals or a child's own room (as in *Goodnight Moon* by Margaret Wise Brown). If children can sense their own world in the pages of your book, they will identify with the story. Editors will be looking for this in your manuscript.

Because picture books have the extra challenge of appealing to both adults and children, picture book editors are looking for books that adults will appreciate as well. Adults are often drawn to books that celebrate a special relationship or have a nostalgic theme. They buy a book for their kids because they see glimpses of their own lives in the subject matter. Karen Ackerman's *Song and Dance Man* and Emily A. McCully's *Mirette on the High Wire*, both Caldecott award winners, are just two examples of this trend in action.

Editors are always looking for a special book that lends a new understanding to life's passages—a child's birth, the arrival of a new sibling, the death of a pet or grandparent. Keep in mind, though, that these are themes that have been played over and over in the picture book market. Editors want fresh approaches to these themes—an inventive twist or a new perspective.

Picture book editors are always looking for fresh manuscripts that deal with timely topics as well. Environmental issues and science themes are two trends that are dominating editors' choices now—and will probably continue to do so in the future. As our world furthers its recognition and celebration of diversity, editors will continue to look for manuscripts that express and promote that diversity.

What Editors Are Not Looking For

In general, most editors are shying away from books that feature talking animals, anthropomorphized creatures, and inanimate objects that somehow take on human characteristics. Of course, there are major exceptions to this rule. Many fine picture books feature characters exactly like these, but they rarely come from first-time authors. In any case, most editors consider this treatment a bit old-fashioned and are moving away from it.

If you do want to use talking animals in your story, you need to take special care in the development of these characters. In general, talking-animal stories fall into two categories: (1) those in which the animals are basically representations of human beings (the Berenstain Bears, for example); and (2) those in which the animals live in their own animal world, interacting as they would in their natural habitat, yet responding in thought and speech very much like human beings. Whether you choose to follow one of these formulas or develop another one, be consistent within your own story.

There are also stories, of course, in which humans and animals interact—a child and his pet, for instance. In these stories, it's generally either the animal's thoughts or the child's thoughts that are revealed to the reader.

Most editors will also quickly reject traditional, tried-and-true picture book themes that have become tired and dated. Picture books featuring little engines that can get up that hill with just a little bit more perseverance will be a difficult sell in today's market. Stories built on "what if" concepts (What if pigs could fly? What if frogs could dance?) will meet the same resistance from editors. You may want to play around with these concepts as writing exercises, but it is doubtful that they will be saleable.

Picture book editors are not looking for stories that hit the readers over the head with a moral or lesson of some kind. That concept may be difficult to put aside, because those are the kinds of stories many of us remember from our childhood. Today's children, though, can see through those thinly veiled morals about good vs. evil and right vs. wrong—and editors can too. Your story should have some redeeming value or feature, but the approach should be subtle.

How to Think Visually

Now comes the hard part—taking your concept and thinking about it as a picture book, complete with effective illustrations. How do you think through your story visually, so you can be sure it fits this category? Here are a few suggestions.

First of all, your story needs to stand completely on its own. Your reader should be able to understand the basics of the plot by simply reading the words you've written. Although the story should succeed on its own, it must also gain visual support from the illustrations or it is not well suited to be a picture book. Think about what kinds of scenes will make good illustrations. Generally speaking, scenes depicting a single activity work well for illustration purposes. Vary your scenes or episodes to allow for variety in the artwork. Strive for fourteen to eighteen scenes per book.

It certainly will help if you have an illustration in mind for each episode in your story. Of course, the editor and illustrator will also have their own ideas. But if you've visualized your story in pictures from beginning to end, you can be certain that it is, indeed, a book that is "illustratable" and an appropriate concept for a picture book. Dummying your book, as suggested earlier, is the best way to ensure that your text has introduced the most effective images for illustration. (Turn to pages 14-15 for instructions on creating a dummy.)

How much visual detail do you add to the text of your story? Add as much as the reader needs to understand the plot. Many beginning writers include too much visual detail because they are trying to control the appearance of the final illustrations. Remember that an illustrator will have his or her own interpretation of the scene—including such things as what your main character looks like, her hair color, how big she is, etc. Unless it is a natural part of the story line, use visual detail sparingly.

Instead, develop other kinds of sensory detail in your plot. Add references to smell, texture, sound and taste if you feel that they will enhance the story. At the same time, don't bog down your plot line with so many details that the reader loses sight of

Breaking With Tradition

There are a number of themes that have been standard fare in the children's book world for so long that they have become tired. If you can come up with a fresh or creative twist on these themes, you may be able to impress an editor. However, if you deal with these plot themes in the same predictable, stale manner, you will probably face a rapid rejection.

- **The Little Engine That Could:** Slush piles are full of stories about a character who, because he or she believes in him or herself, achieves success. They are trite and have become passé.
- **Runt of the Litter:** This kind of story generally involves an underdog who somehow overcomes his or her odds to achieve success. Again, this plotline is overdone and trite. This type of story will find its way back into your SASE (self-addressed, stamped envelope) quickly.
- **It Was All a Dream:** In this story, a character usually experiences an incredible adventure fraught with danger, and then wakes up in his own bed to discover it was only a dream. Frequently there is ambiguity at the story's end as to whether the episode really was a dream, as when Dorothy recognizes the characters at the end of the *Wizard of Oz* or when the child in *The Polar Express* by Chris Van Allsburg wakes to find the bell under the tree. This kind of story is also overdone and, unless it comes from a skilled, well-known author, is likely to meet rejection.
- **What If . . . ?** Such stories involve characters, usually animals, who want a trait they don't have—a frog who wants to fly, for example. Generally, when the creature gains his desired trait, it isn't all it was cracked up to be and he wants to return to his former self. While this kind of plot is the least exhausted of the five, it is still overused and a risky proposition.
- **Risk-Takers:** This plot usually involves a character, often an animal or an inanimate object with human qualities, who is bored with the confines of his home. He heads out in search of adventure, comes up with more than he bargained for and ends up vowing never to take such risks again. *The Tale of Peter Rabbit* relies on this particular plot device. The plot is dated and trite, and also suggests something not entirely positive to children about taking risks.

where the plot is going. Your details should occur naturally in the story and not seem contrived.

Plotting

Thinking visually and considering the plot of your story go hand in hand. Your story should build appropriately and be resolved effectively as in all good fiction.

The first thing you want to do in your picture book is introduce the conflict—in the story's opening lines. Many beginning writers make the mistake of introducing the story's main character in detail, telling the reader her age, hair color and family history before ever discussing her real problem. Consider these two opening passages for a picture book:

> Jamie was a mischievous kindergartner with a wide, toothy grin and a ready smile.
>
> Jamie was a mischief maker—and mischief was causing him one big problem in his kindergarten class.

The first opening line introduces the character, but doesn't reveal any real urgency about the story at hand. The second sentence suggests that Jamie has a problem that needs to be solved. The reader will be engaged by what the problem is and how Jamie will solve it.

After you've identified your character's problem—and only after that point—you can work in details about the character's life if you feel they are necessary for your reader to understand the story. If those details break up the story's flow or slow it down, they probably don't need to be included.

In the middle of your story, you want to show how your character struggles with solving his problem. It may be helpful to think of the middle of your story in three episodes. During the first episode, the character tries one method to solve the problem, and that method either fails entirely or moves the character a bit closer to the goal. The second episode, which should involve a more difficult strategy than the first, should move the character closer to the final goal, but that goal should still be out of reach. The final episode should involve the most difficult task and should be so challenging that the character almost fails to achieve that goal. In fact, he *may* fail entirely to reach his intended goal, but gain something else instead. Or he may actually reach the intended goal and discover it wasn't all that he thought it would be. Either way, the last episode must involve real struggle. The reader needs to question whether the character will actually achieve what he set out to do, and that question is what will captivate your reader to the last line of the story.

It's not enough for the main character to simply achieve his or her goal. By facing the obstacles in the story and overcoming them, the main character needs to be transformed in an important and significant way. At the end of your picture book, it is appropriate to sum up that character growth. Reinforce the fact that your character achieved the goal and share the character's reaction with the reader. Then end your story quickly and tie the ending to your story's beginning. (You can find a visual representation of how this works on page 23.)

Vocabulary and Readabilty

How much do I have to worry about word choice and reading level? Do I need to refer to a word list? Is this language too advanced for my audience? These questions often confound—and even paralyze—the beginning picture book writer, but the answers aren't as difficult as they may seem.

Referring to a controlled vocabulary list is probably not necessary, unless, of course, you are writing for a textbook or educational publisher. Instead, make sure that your story line is understandable to the reader. This advice doesn't always suggest that every word be understood and easily read by children of the right age level, especially since picture books are usually read aloud to children. However, it does mean selecting words that can be understood in context, even if they are long words that a child might not be able to define.

Let's take the word *elegant*. It's a rather "adult" word, a word that most kids wouldn't use in speech or understand if asked the

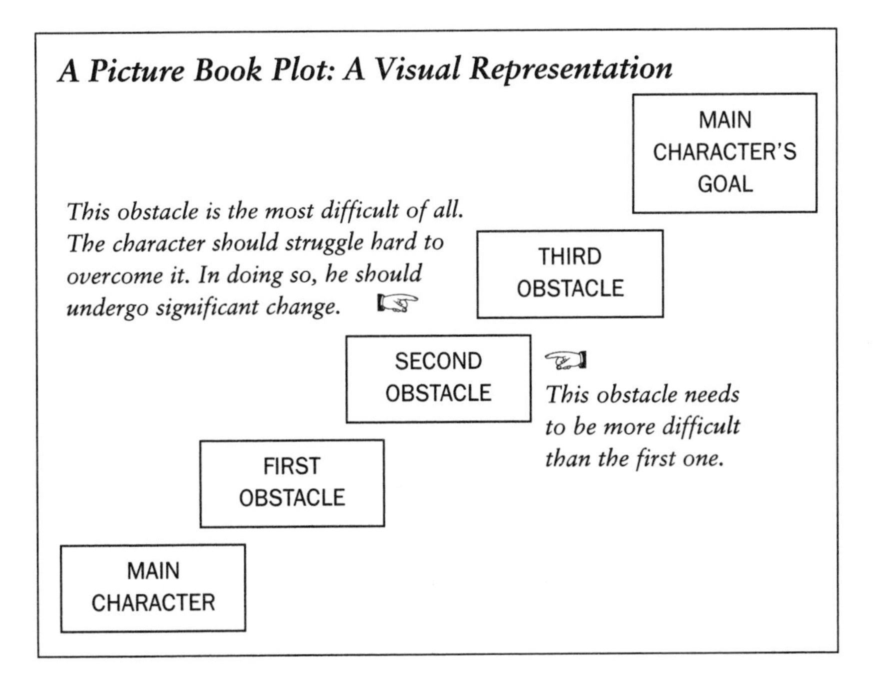

meaning. But if you use it in context, as in the phrase *the elegant green dress made Cinderella feel more beautiful than ever*, your readers will understand the word's meaning. Even if they don't fully understand the term, they really don't need to know the word to understand the rest of the story.

The point is not to fret over things like simple word choices. Introduce a context for the more difficult vocabulary words if you can. And never use a difficult word or concept, without explanation, that is necessary to the understanding of the story's plot line.

Remember that children take a real delight in a creative and playful use of language. Don't be afraid to play with different sounds and sound combinations. When I wrote *Annabelle's Awful Waffle*, an add-on story about a little girl who adds all kinds of crazy toppings to her waffle, I had great fun coming up with the toppings. I chose my toppings, which ranged from spinach to cherries to popcorn, both for their "gross" factor and because of the way they sounded. At the end of the story, the toppings "topple" off the waffle. I chose the word *topple*, instead of the more simple word *fall*, because I liked the way it sounded with *waffle* and *awful.* And don't hesitate to make up a word or use a less-than-standard variation of a word if it can be understood in context.

There are ways to make your book more reader-friendly. Using shorter sentences usually helps. When using longer sentences, take care to divide them into shorter phrases or clauses. Sentence fragments are also appropriate in picture books if they are used for effect. Introduce paragraph breaks more frequently than you would in material that you would write for adults.

Also remember that repetition is a great way to reinforce a story's plot and enhance its readability. Repeating difficult words, or entire phrases with difficult words, is one way to lend understanding to the plot and to help children develop reading skills.

How Can You Test Whether Your Picture Book Is Ready to Go?

When I was an editor, I often received manuscripts with cover letters urging me to consider a story because "my children loved it" or "my daughter's class had nothing but good things to say." Those are treasured compliments, to be sure, but remember that kids frequently tell you what you want to hear. And your own children will certainly respond positively to a story they believe may have been written just for them.

How, then, do you test market your idea? How do you take your picture book manuscript for a test drive?

The first way is to read it out loud—to yourself—listening for awkward phrases, slips of the tongue, and the like. After you've tried that, read it aloud into a tape recorder and play it back to yourself. Again, note awkward spots, spots where your mind wanders, places where your tongue trips.

The next step is to try it out on a trusted adult—preferably someone who knows children's literature. If you are a member of a writer's group, that's a good place to start. You might also try a teacher or a children's librarian at your local library. And you may be lucky enough to have a children's writer or instructor in your community who mentors emerging writers. Keep in mind that these people are professionals. Offer to pay them for their advice. At

To Rhyme or Not to Rhyme

There is a general belief that editors of picture books prefer manuscripts that don't rhyme. The objection, though, is not usually to the use of rhyme itself. It is to poorly constructed, awkwardly written verse. If writers were completely honest with themselves, many of them would have to admit that they choose to write in verse because they are simply not comfortable with prose. But rhyme is much more difficult to master—and involves much more than simply finding the right "rhyme" for a particular word. It requires an understanding of the rhythms of poetry, the use of rhyme scheme and the ability to create rhyme that doesn't sound forced or unnatural.

If you really want to use rhyme in your story, you need to ask yourself some hard questions:

- Does rhyme enhance the story?
- Does rhyme come easily to you?
- Is there rhythm and meter to back up the rhyme (and can you document that rhythm by coming up with a pattern of stressed and unstressed syllables)?
- Does the rhyme make the story sound trivial in any way?
- Could the same story be told just as well in prose rather than in verse?

If the answer to the last question is yes, you will probably be more likely to sell the story if you write in prose.

the very least, you should offer some token of thanks or some exchange—with a librarian, you may offer a volunteer session shelving books, for instance.

And then, if you feel you are ready, it's time to try your story out on the kids who will be your readers. Here, you need to tread carefully. As I've said, kids often tell you what you want to hear. Instead of reading the book aloud yourself, try asking a friend or a teacher or a librarian to read it aloud to a group of kids at a story hour. Sit in the back and watch carefully.

As the writer, of course, you want your audience to love your story, but praise is not what you are looking for at this point. You are looking for your readers' reactions. Do they seem bored? Are they excited at the appropriate times? Do they laugh when they are supposed to? Are they satisfied with the story's ending? Are they intrigued by the story's title? By carefully observing children listening to your story, you can learn invaluable things about your story's pacing, subject matter, conflict and marketability.

At the end, ask (or have the teacher ask) the kids some questions about the book. Instead of asking the question that is probably burning in your mind—Did you like it?—ask the kids to repeat the story's basic plot back to you. From their response, you will see if they "got it," if the story did what you intended it to do.

Some Words From the Heart

By now you must be sighing and muttering to yourself, "I never knew that there were so many rules." It's true that all of these requirements may seem a bit overwhelming, but they are meant only as general guidelines, not hard and fast commandments.

Keep in mind that all of the restrictions need to be balanced with your personal view of what you think picture books should offer children. You also need to consider your personal needs as a writer—not just as a writer for children.

My picture books have followed these so-called rules, but they also directly reflected something that was going on in my own life. *Grandpa's Magic* is about a little girl who enjoys taking long walks with her arthritic grandfather, but it is also about the way I came to terms with my grandfather's aging. On the surface, *Annabelle's Awful Waffle* is a book about a little girl who puts too many toppings on her waffles, but it is really about the differences between siblings. And *Whatever I Do, the Monster Does Too* tells the story of a little boy who is frightened by a monster underneath his own bed, but it is really about the way I overcome and ultimately embrace my own fears.

Your goals as a writer may be different from mine, but remember that all good writing comes from the heart. Don't let these picture book rules and restrictions get in your way. Picture books are fun—fun to read and fun to write. The best way to become a successful writer is to feel good about what you write and to have fun doing it.

Tips From the Top

1. Consider the various features of your manuscript. Does it appeal to both adults and young readers? Could it be used in a classroom? Does it teach a particular concept or deal with a transition with which young readers typically struggle? The more of these features your manuscript has, the better its chance to reach a broad audience.

2. Make sure that you are writing for the "average" child and adult reader. While your story should stretch your readers' imaginations, it shouldn't stretch their ability to understand the story's concepts.

3. If your story has a religious or moral message, consider approaching a religious publishing house.

4. Evaluate your idea for a picture book carefully and make sure it has enough breadth and depth for a book. Put another way, is the story "big enough" to be a book? If it's very simple and extremely short, your story may work better as a magazine story, for instance.

5. Refer to publishers' guidelines carefully and make sure that your story fits the type of titles they are currently publishing. (You can receive the guidelines by writing the publisher and requesting them, enclosing a self-addressed stamped envelope, or SASE. For more information on how to request guidelines, see pages 73-74.)

6. Spend some time coming up with a playful and creative title that will pique an editor's imagination. An eye-catching title—one that is intriguing but doesn't give the story away—is a terrific way to move your manuscript higher up on the slush pile.

7. If you have tested your story out on some young readers, it is acceptable to tell an editor that you've done so. Avoid exaggeration, though. Phrases like "My own children adored the story" and "I received praise from my daughter's class and her teacher for my story" can sound trite and overused, and they carry little real weight with an editor.

8. Send the dummy along *only* if the guidelines state that it is acceptable.

Inspiration Exercises

1. Make a list of things that kids are concerned about when they are prime picture book age (preschool through second grade). Select five or six that have meaning for you and jot each down on a separate note card. Now think about the way you might deal with those issues in a picture book plot. Jot down notes on the note cards for future book ideas.

2. Select a favorite fairy tale and try to tell it from a different character's perspective. You may also combine several fairy tales into one. What would happen if Cinderella encountered Snow White? What if the Big Bad Wolf had come across Goldilocks instead of the three little pigs? Play out these possibilities in your head or on paper.

3. Research a folk tale from another culture. Consider ways that the folk tale could be retold in picture book form.

4. Select a topic that is routinely taught in kindergarten, first or second grade (dinosaurs, insects, ocean creatures and the rain forest are some possibilities). Write a fictional story about the topic that introduces some "hard" facts.

5. Consider how the concept of reversal might work in a picture book story. What would a monster be like if he were good? How about a witch who wanted to be friendly?

6. Consider what would happen if a character accepted the ridiculous as real. (Amelia Bedelia, the wacky housekeeper in Peggy Parish's classic series, relies on just this device.)

7. Select your favorite picture book and look at it critically. Consider these elements:

- How does the book focus on a child-centered conflict?
- How does the book introduce the familiar aspects of a child's world?
- How does the book allow the main character to solve the story's problem?
- How does the book deal with words that might not be understood by the child reader/listener?
- How does the book appeal on two levels—to the adult market and the child audience?

8. Choose an average-length picture book and retype it. Without referring to the original, dummy the book as if it were your own. Have you paced the book as the original was paced? Is your version better than the original? If your version is different from the original one, how will the illustrations change as a result?

3 BEGINNING READERS, CHAPTER BOOKS AND NOVELS

"I can read!"

That's the triumphant cry of an elementary-school-age child who has begun to master the reading process. It's an exciting time for children. For the first time, they can enter the world that an author created for them on their own. They meet the characters face to face. They become part of the story.

For most young readers, the feeling is absolutely exhilarating. And, if you write for these emerging readers, the experience is equally so. After all, you are helping nurture that reader. You are, in fact, inspiring lifelong reading habits.

The Market and the Audience

There are three broad categories of books for the elementary-school-age reader.

- **Easy readers** are aimed at emergent readers in kindergarten, first and second grade. These books are illustrated either in black and white or in color with pictures that provide reading cues. They are designed for children to read to themselves either silently or out loud. Children may select these books on their own, but they probably do so with the help or advice of teachers or parents. Adults are still a part of both the audience and the market for these books.

• **Chapter books** are carefully designed to bridge the gap between picture books and novels. They are aimed at slightly more confident readers, who may also be in the first, second or third grade. The reading level varies for chapter books, but most chapter books are aimed at readers who can sustain interest in a longer plot. Most readers select chapter books on their own, but they may still receive some adult guidance.

• **Middle grade novels** become popular in the middle grade years (third through sixth grade), sometimes called the "golden age of the reader." Kids this age are developing an unprecedented enthusiasm for reading. They are hungry for books, and many devour them title after title. Part of their enthusiasm comes from the fact that they are seeing their lives mirrored in the stories they read. Books become their companions, helping and humoring them through the trials of growing up.

The hunger for books in the middle grades also comes from readers selecting their own books for the first time in their lives. This newfound independence fuels their enthusiasm. While adults may be giving advice on what kids should read in the middle grades, they aren't controlling their selections.

Middle grade readers are making reading decisions based not only on their own taste, but on the recommendations of friends. Certain books and subjects simply become fashionable in the middle grades and, like styles of clothing, they tend to dominate the market for a concentrated period of time. Some middle grade series that were fashionable in their time include Sweet Valley Twins, The Baby-Sitter's Club, and Goosebumps.

The middle grade years are also the first time that distinctions are made between "girl books" and "boy books." Generally at this age, boys want to read about boys and girls want to read about girls. In earlier years, these preferences were not all that important. And, in spite of the progress that has been made in equality of the sexes, subject matter is still divided along traditional gender lines: Boys' books tend to be about sports, science and other traditional boy topics; girls' books tend to be about friendship issues, pets (horses are still popular), the arts, and sports that girls have traditionally participated in, like gymnastics and swimming.

The Form, Length and Structure

While each of the book categories has its own standards for length and style, easy readers, chapter books and middle grade novels do have several things in common:

- They look older and more sophisticated than picture books. Most children who are beginning to master reading want "real books" instead of picture books, which they view as "babyish." To reflect this new level of sophistication, books for emerging readers are usually about the same size as books for older readers and feature cover illustrations that are realistic in style.
- They have single characters as their heroes and are told through this character's viewpoint. Usually, this character is a kid who is dealing with a typical kid situation—often a similar situation to one that the reader might be dealing with.
- They center on a problem and a character who solves that problem, much as picture books do. Middle grade readers are, as a rule, more problem driven than easy readers and chapter books.
- They are full of action that the reader can visualize. Chapter books and middle grade readers may or may not be illustrated, but they all rely heavily on visual action.
- They use humor as part of their plot line.
- They are written in a highly kid-appealing style. The voice the author uses is typically both lighthearted and intimate.

Most publishers have their own specifications for the lengths of each of these various types of books, and the best information comes from the publisher's own guidelines. (Publishers generally provide guidelines for writers that state length and subject requirements. You'll find more information about guidelines and a sample letter requesting them on pages 73-74.) The standard lengths and formats are listed below. When figuring the length of your book manuscripts, estimate an average of 250 words per page.

- Easy readers are illustrated in color or black and white, and the illustrations are designed to provide the reader with cues to help master reading the story. Most easy readers are about 1,000 to 1,500 words. In bound form, they run from 40 to 64 pages.
- Chapter books may or may not be illustrated. If they are illustrated, the illustrations are generally simple black-and-white drawings. The length of these books is determined by the age and reading level of the reader, and can run anywhere from 1,500 to 10,000 words or so. In book length they generally run 40 to 80 pages.
- Middle grade novels are less likely to be illustrated than the other two categories and are read primarily by readers older than third grade. They run anywhere from 64 to 120 pages, or 10,000 to 16,000 words, and contain between eight and sixteen chapters.

Subjects

The majority of early readers, chapter books and middle grade readers concern subjects and conflicts familiar to readers of this age. Popular topics include sibling rivalry, pets, and family and friendship issues. Many plots take place in school settings and emphasize routines that are much like the reader's own school experience.

With some notable exceptions (*Charlotte's Web* by E.B. White comes immediately to mind), books for beginning readers are rarely about animal characters. Instead, the characters in these books are kids themselves, usually the same age or just slightly older than the intended audience. A child main character, perhaps with some adult advice but *not* intervention, generally solves the story's problem.

Several genres are popular in this category.

Mysteries have always been popular among middle grade readers, and this popularity has filtered down to chapter books and easy readers. These books usually feature kid detectives who solve some sort of mystery through their own intuition and intelligence. The mysteries themselves are somewhat complicated, but generally don't involve real crimes or dangerous situations, especially for lower-age levels. Publishers are always looking for mysteries, but keep in mind that mysteries are extremely difficult to write and require both effective plot structure and well-defined character growth.

Fantasy is another genre that has deep roots in the middle grade age group, but, unlike mysteries, it is primarily a middle grade phenomenon. Most fantasies for middle grade readers involve magical situations in which the main character—again, usually a kid—who is empowered in some way. Some of the favorites feature kids who demonstrate power over adults, like Roald Dahl's *Matilda*.

The Little House series of books, written by Laura Ingalls Wilder, is probably the most popular example of middle grade historical fiction. This category has seen a resurgence inspired by the American Girl series of books. These novels all feature historically accurate fiction; each one is about a different girl and is set in a different era of American history. Other publishers have followed suit with their own series, most of them featuring a young fictional character in a different historical setting in each title.

And then, of course, there is horror. The controversial children's horror genre, popularized by R.L. Stine, dominated middle grade readers for over ten years before finally burning out. It even filtered down to the chapter book level. It is doubtful, however, that true horror will filter all the way down to easy readers. The subject matter is simply too objectionable for first and second graders.

Series Books

Series books also have a long tradition in juvenile publishing—dating from the days of Cherry Ames, the Bobbsey Twins, the Hardy Boys and Nancy Drew. Series appeal to middle grade readers because there's a sense of reliability. The characters are familiar, the plots are similar, and the readers know that if they liked one book in the series, they will probably like the others.

There's another reason series are popular with middle grade readers: collectability. Young readers generally like to collect books in a series, buying each one until their collection is complete or until they grow out of the series.

Also consider that most series books are published in paperback, priced nicely within allowance range. Affordability enables middle grade readers to make their own reading decisions and purchase those books with their own money. That increases the pride in ownership and reading enthusiasm.

All of this is good news for writers and for publishers. Young readers will buy series books because of their collectability, while they might not buy single titles. (They will check these out of the library instead.) Series books are also popular among book fairs and book clubs (marketed through classrooms as fund-raisers), and this means huge potential sales to publishers.

For that reason, publishers are frequently looking for new and fresh concepts for series. Some are even looking for writers to ghostwrite books in an existing series. If you are interested in pursuing a series idea, study the series concepts currently on the market. Then, the best rule of thumb is to write a single novel with characters who have enough depth and potential to be "continued" in future books. Prepare outlines for those future titles in the series and submit them with the manuscript of your completed novel. (Publishers may differ in their requirements for series proposals. Be sure to check their guidelines.)

Plotting

There is no secret formula to plotting books for young readers, but there are some general rules to keep in mind.

Easy readers usually have clear, simple plots that are sometimes even a bit predictable. There are rarely subplots, nor is there a real "edge of your seat" quality to the pacing of the story. The conflict is usually not of a serious nature and reflects the kind of conflicts kids that age are dealing with—losing a tooth, wanting a pet or dealing with a fear. Extraneous detail—such as character and setting description—is minimal. Easy readers are usually packed with action that propels the plot forward and keeps the reader interested.

As their name suggests, chapter books are broken into short chapters (three to four book pages or less), each with its own episode. Chapter books may be developed in one of two ways. The first is with a traditional plot line, where each episode works to further resolve the story's conflict. In the second format, each of the chapters is self-contained but loosely connected to the story

Some Great Examples to Guide Your Writing

EARLY READERS:

The Cat in the Hat and *The Cat in the Hat Comes Back*, Dr. Seuss
Chester, Syd Hoff
Four on the Shore, Edward Marshall
Frog and Toad, Arnold Lobel
In A Dark, Dark Room, Alvin Schwartz
Leo, Zack and Emmie, Amy Ehrlich

EARLY READER SERIES:

Nate the Great series, Marjorie Sharmat

CHAPTER BOOKS

Amber Brown is Not A Crayon (and sequels), Paula Danziger
Ramona Quimby (and sequels), Beverly Cleary

CHAPTER BOOK SERIES:

Amelia Bedelia series, Peggy Parish
Baby-Sitter's Little Sister series, Ann M. Martin
Fox series, Edward Marshall
Henry and Mudge series, Cynthia Rylant
Kids of the Polk Street School series, Patricia Reilly Giff
Leo and Emily series, Franz Brandenberg

MIDDLE GRADE NOVELS:

Anastasia Krupnik (and sequels), Lois Lowry
Bunnicula and *Howliday Inn*, Deborah and James Howe
Class Clown, *Teacher's Pet* and *Class President*, Johanna Hurwitz
Fourth Grade Rats, Jerry Spinelli
Harriet the Spy, Louise Fitzhugh
My Teacher Fried My Brains (and sequels), Bruce Coville
The Plant That Ate Dirty Socks (and sequels), Nancy McArthur
Shiloh, Phyllis Reynolds Naylor
Superfudge and *Tales of a Fourth Grade Nothing*, Judy Blume

FANTASY:

Bridge to Terabithia, Katherine Paterson
Castle in the Attic, Elizabeth Winthrop
Charlie and the Chocolate Factory and *Matilda*, Roald Dahl
Ralph S. Mouse, Beverly Cleary
A Wrinkle in Time, Madeleine L'Engle

MYSTERIES:

The Case of the Baker Street Irregular and *The Case of the Vanishing Corpse*, Robert Newman
Dollhouse Murders, Betty Ren Wright
Encyclopedia Brown series, Donald J. Sobol
Wait Till Helen Comes, Mary Downing Hahn

HISTORICAL:

Baby and *Sarah, Plain and Tall*, Patricia MacLachlan
Borrowed Children, George-Ella Lyon
Catherine, Called Birdy, Karen Cushman
Little House series, Laura Ingalls Wilder
Number the Stars, Lois Lowry
American Girl series, various authors

MIDDLE GRADE SERIES:

Boxcar Children series, Gertrude Chandler Warner
Baby-Sitter's Club series, Ann M. Martin
Bailey School Kids series, Debbie Dadey and Marcia Thornton Jones
Goosebumps series, R.L. Stine
Animorphs series, K.A. Applegate

PLEASE NOTE: This list barely scratches the surface. For more examples, ask your librarian, a teacher or some children.

that precedes it. In chapter books, as in easy readers, the conflict is usually not serious and is one that the readers of the books may be dealing with themselves.

Not surprisingly, middle grade novels have the most complicated plots of the three. Their plots are driven by a problem or conflict, and that conflict should be introduced early on—in the first paragraph, if possible, and definitely in the first chapter. In middle grade novels, there may be a subplot or two, but the main conflict-driven plot is the controlling force in the story.

The conflicts in middle grade novels are generally of the lighter variety (centered on school situations, friendship and changes in home life) but may also be more hard-hitting (death, dealing with differences, dealing with moral dilemmas, etc.). Keep in mind that even though you may be dealing with a conflict that many adults would find trivial, as a writer for children you need to take that conflict seriously.

There is more descriptive detail introduced in a middle grade novel than in books for younger readers. Readers will want to know more about what characters look like, how old they are, what the setting is like and so on. Remember that these details are secondary to the conflict. Conflict is what propels the plot, and every single episode in the story must relate to that conflict in some real way.

Middle grade novels also rely heavily on visual action—often humorous visual action—to enliven the plot. One way to ensure you have enough visual action in your plot is to ask yourself if you can think of at least one illustration that can be created for each chapter. Even though middle grade books aren't always illustrated, this exercise will help you make sure that your story has enough visual appeal.

Another helpful plotting device for middle grade novels is to think of each chapter as having three distinct episodes, each one moving the plot forward. These episodes may involve a change of scene—from the breakfast table to school to a character's bedroom, for example—and they should be distinct from each other.

These distinct scenes should be connected by carefully crafted transitions, passages that act as bridges from scene to scene. Transitions are extremely important to middle grade readers. While readers at this level have mastered much of the reading process, they may still be struggling with comprehension. Reminding them where they are in time and place is one way to keep them grounded and involved in the story.

Characters

Young readers demand genuine kid characters in their books, characters who seem quite familiar to them and who they feel comfortable with. The characters you create should have the same flaws and the same reactions that most kids do. Many writers make the mistake of creating characters who are "larger than life" or who are too good to be believed. Keep in mind that kids—like adults—

aren't perfect human beings, and your characters shouldn't be either.

In all categories of children's fiction, the story's main character needs to be the most fully developed. It is this character who should demonstrate growth and change by the end of the story. For that reason, you need to spend time really getting to know this character—how he reacts, how he speaks, his likes and dislikes.

Obviously, there should be other characters in your novel too. These secondary characters should most often be the other kid characters with whom your main character is interacting—her friends, classmates or siblings.

There is usually a *small* cast of adults who also make an appearance in the story. The adults should be admirable in some way. They can have typical human flaws, but they are usually honest and reliable characters. For instance, a teacher can have quirks, but he should not be evil or unlikable. And, as in picture books, adult intervention needs to be kept to a minimum.

The Role of Humor

Humor is extremely important to young readers. While they enjoy seeing reflections of themselves in stories, they especially like stories that make light of their own situations. That doesn't mean you should make fun of them. It does mean that you should recreate an experience in a way that allows readers to laugh at themselves. It's a fine line, but the best writers for school-age readers walk that line very well.

What kind of humor works best? The kinds of things that make kids laugh—visual gags, corny jokes, ridiculous situations, snappy dialogue—are all ways to work humor into a story. And while writers should not employ humor at the expense of their readers, they can poke fun at their other characters—siblings, for instance, who can do wacky, gross or embarrassing things.

Within the bounds of reasonable taste, the situations in books for young readers can be a bit gross. Depending on the publisher, writers can sprinkle their stories with humor considered tasteless humor (at least by adult standards)—picking one's nose, for instance, or mixing up a wild and unappetizing concoction. For an example of this kind of humor, take a look at Judy Blume's *Tales of a Fourth Grade Nothing*; in this book, a younger sibling actually swallows his older brother's pet turtle!

A word of caution: Young readers find sarcasm difficult to process when read. This may seem surprising since they use sarcasm all the time in their speech. Still, when reading, young readers process sarcasm literally instead of sarcastically. When using sarcasm for young readers, it is best to identify it as such by using tag phrases like *in a voice dripping with sarcasm* or *she said, jokingly.*

The Role of Dialogue

Young readers expect dialogue as part of their stories. For one thing, dialogue creates white space. It makes a page of type look less dense and more inviting to the reader. Secondly, young readers live in a world of dialogue. They make sense of their own world, in part, because of the way they process things that are said to them. And, finally, dialogue is one way to further define your characters for your reader.

But dialogue should be used carefully in books for young readers. The role of dialogue is to move the plot forward in some significant way. The dialogue polite people exchange when they meet is appropriate in that context, but characters in a story don't need to make polite conversation. They need to say things that advance the plot and deal directly with the story's conflict.

When using dialogue for young readers, you need to identify your speaker regularly. Make sure your reader knows who is speaking and when a different character has begun his part of the conversation. Use tag lines, such as *he said* and *she said*, to indicate your speaker. And be sure to begin a new paragraph every time a different character is speaking. (See chapter five for more on punctuating dialogue.)

It is also important to break up passages of dialogue. When people speak, they pause, gesture and reflect. Your characters need to do the same. Avoid long speeches that aren't broken up. They aren't natural, and they are difficult to read.

Internal dialogue, the way a character speaks to him or herself, is as important as actual dialogue, especially for middle grade readers. This internal dialogue can often give the reader the sense of how the main character is working out the conflict, and can create a sense of intimacy with the reader. (Internal dialogue is punctuated differently than dialogue that is spoken out loud. See chapter five, page 67 for specific guidelines.)

Vocabulary and Readability

The questions of readability and vocabulary choice are issues that writers for young readers struggle with just as much as picture book writers do. With young readers, though, the question is perhaps more critical. What kind of words can the readers actually read? What can they comprehend and understand?

Once again, I urge writers to avoid word lists and readability tests. Instead, rely on repetition, intuition and context to guide your word choices and help the reader to understand the story.

Here are some simple rules to help guide you in word choice and readability:

- Rely on short, unencumbered sentences without a lot of extraneous clauses. When I was an editor, we had a rule: In books for young readers (chapter books, easy readers or middle grade novels), sentences should be an average of ten words long. As arbitrary as it sounds, by using this guideline, I was often able to identify convoluted sentences and awkward sentence structure. You might want to apply this rule to your own writing. If you have a number of sentences that exceed this length, your sentence structure may be too complicated for your reader, especially for younger readers.
- Make sure that you have a good balance between "white space" and dense text. Dialogue, short paragraphs and longer paragraphs should be interspersed, so the page looks inviting rather than overwhelming to the beginning reader.
- If there is a simpler word that means the same thing, use it! Refer to a thesaurus for word choice options. *The Children's Writer's Word Book*, a thesaurus organized by grade level, is an excellent resource for writers who are unsure about word choice and reading level.
- If you are introducing a more difficult word, use it several times in a row in context so the reader can glean its meaning. Repetition is one way children master reading. Especially for the

lower grades, repetition can be used to establish a rhythm and an understanding of your story.

Know Your Audience

More than any other category of children's books, writing for young readers requires that you really know kids—what they think, how they talk, how they perceive the world and their place in it, and what their own conflicts, aspirations and interests are. No discussion of guidelines or list of rules can substitute for that knowledge.

If you are around kids every day, you probably know more than you think about writing for them. Learn to rely on your intuition and feelings about them. They are your best source of information and inspiration.

If you aren't around kids, find a way to get involved with them. Volunteer at a school, a church or a recreation center. Talk to them, play with them, get to know them, learn to care about them.

Then you will be ready to give them the best gift of all—books that will enrich their lives.

Tips From the Top

1. Know your audience. Know what issues elementary-school-age kids are dealing with at various grade levels. Learn how these issues vary from boys to girls.
2. Choose characters who are your readers' age or a bit older. Make sure they are authentic, believable and likable.
3. Avoid stereotyped characters—the school bully, for instance.
4. Learn about the developmental differences between girls and boys of elementary school age.
5. Choose subject matter with which your readers can identify.
6. Use dialogue to move your plot forward. Make sure your dialogue sounds natural and contemporary.
7. Unless it has a historical setting, make sure your story sounds contemporary. The plot should have a contemporary problem, your characters should speak in contemporary style and the characters

themselves should seem as if they could live in today's world.

8. Learn the market for your particular genre. Make sure your story fits the appropriate length requirements and subject guidelines. (For more about information on researching the market, see chapter six.)

9. For early readers and chapter books, don't overlook folk, tall and fairy tales as sources of inspiration. These subjects would be less likely to sell as novels for middle grade readers.

Inspiration Exercises

1. Take a favorite fairy tale and rewrite it as an easy reader and a chapter book.

2. Write down some momentous occasions in the lives of elementary school children. Losing a tooth, learning to whistle or ride a bicycle, and moving are just some examples. Choose several and develop a story line based on them.

3. Locate a passage of stylized dialogue, perhaps from a Charles Dickens or a Louisa May Alcott novel. Rewrite the dialogue as today's kids would speak it.

4. Observe two or more kids interacting. Select one of those kids as a main character and write a short story inspired by what you observed.

5. Read a middle grade novel. Identify the way the plot is developed. How many episodes are there per chapter? How many scene changes? Is there a subplot? How many adults are in the story? What role do they play? When is the conflict introduced?

6. Read an easy reader. Consider carefully the way more difficult words are introduced. Has the author used repetition to suggest meaning? Has the author introduced the words in context?

7. Read a chapter book. Study the way the book is organized. Is each chapter its own story or do they build upon each other?

4 NONFICTION

Most writers—not just those who write for children—dream of writing fiction. In fact, the pursuit of the "great American novel" is almost synonymous with pursuing a writing career. But those who hold fast to this dream are, quite simply, less likely to realize it. That's because there is a much larger market for nonfiction than for fiction. This is true of adult literature as well as children's books. The reason is simple: There are many more nonfiction books being published today than fiction.

That's great news for the beginning writer who is open to this creative and exciting genre. Writing nonfiction books is a terrific way to break into the field. And, because nonfiction books are most often bought on the basis of a proposal instead of a manuscript, the time and risk involved for the writer is actually less. (For more on what is involved in writing a proposal, see chapter seven.)

Where do you start to come up with ideas for nonfiction books? The best place to start is with your own experience. Do you have an interest in a certain area or field? Is this subject appealing to kids or could you make it so? Do you have special knowledge or inside information about a topic of interest to a publisher and to kids? Once you start thinking about your own range of experience and interests, you'll probably become even more excited about the opportunities nonfiction has to offer.

The Creative Nature of Nonfiction

When many of us think about nonfiction for kids, we think of the drab, textbook-style books that we used for school research and reports when we were younger. Today's nonfiction is much more lively. It demands an approach that tackles the subject in a direct but creative way, an approach that needs to be both kid-appealing and age appropriate.

Let me offer an example from my own writing. After a field trip with my daughter's class to our local zoo's artificial coral reef exhibit, I became fascinated with the topic. For one thing, the coral reef supports a wider variety of plant and animal life than practically any other place on earth, with the possible exception of the rain forest. Secondly, the topic offered many teaching opportunities. By exploring the coral reef, young readers could learn about such topics as the food chain, symbiosis, protective coloration and camouflage, to name only a few. I knew I had a great idea for a nonfiction trade book and thought it would have marketing opportunities in schools and libraries as well.

But I struggled with one problem. How do I explain this complicated habitat in a way that young children—say first and second graders—can understand?

Then I hit on it! I could describe the coral reef as a kind of underwater neighborhood. While it is quite different from the neighborhoods kids live in, there are enough similarities to make it an effective metaphor. Once I found an approach that was both kid-appealing and creative, I knew I was onto something. *A Look Around a Coral Reef* not only sold to a publisher but was well received by teachers, librarians and kids.

As a writer, I found the process every bit as creative and rewarding as writing picture books or longer fiction.

What Is Good Nonfiction?

Good nonfiction for children is admirable for the same reasons as good fiction—it features interesting characters, is appropriate to the audience and it promotes a sense of power through the knowledge it imparts. Good nonfiction, in fact, has the flavor of fiction. There is a sense of storytelling and discovery in every single sentence.

But most of all, good nonfiction is impeccably researched. The facts are checked over and over against several reliable sources.

Not only does the information in a nonfiction book need to be checked, the information not included must be reviewed as well. The writer needs to make sure that she includes all the facts a reader needs to understand the topic. It's easy to omit important information, and a nonfiction writer can't afford to gloss over essential details that the reader needs to fully understand the topic.

The Market and the Audience

Unlike picture books, chapter books and beginning readers, the audience for almost all nonfiction books includes kids, parents, teachers and especially librarians. Kids are looking for ways to acquire information either for their own use or for school projects. Parents, teachers and librarians are looking for ways to help them do that easily.

Readability is more important when writing nonfiction books. Some publishers even do official readability tests on their books. Again, don't become overly concerned about readability. If your word processing program or writing software can determine readability for you, though, it's a good idea to run it and see if your manuscript is at least in the ball park.

If you don't have access to a readability program, you can do a number of simple things to make sure your manuscript can be understood by your reader. First of all, make good use of your thesaurus. If there is a simpler word that means the same thing as the word you've chosen, use it. (Again, the *Children's Writer's Word Book* is an excellent resource for improving readability.)

You can define key words when they are introduced and/or in a glossary. It's also a good idea to provide a phonetic pronunciation so the readers will recognize the word when they hear it again.

Finally, develop a writing style that is lively and engaging but direct. It is important to be straightforward and not to present information in a way that may be misunderstood by the reader.

Types of Nonfiction Books

Nonfiction books are published in a picture book format for prereaders and beginning readers, and as books with chapters or sections for older readers. Most nonfiction picture books fit the length restrictions of fiction picture books, although some may run a bit longer than 32 pages. Nonfiction books for older readers also usually run the same length as their fiction counterparts.

There is such a wide variety of nonfiction books being published that I would be oversimplifying the genre to list its various categories. Still, this brief and admittedly incomplete list will acquaint you with some existing categories and should get your ideas flowing.

- **Biographies** are one of the most popular nonfiction categories and they are offered at every grade level—even as easy readers and picture books. Biographies of famous Americans, sports figures, heroes and writers are always in demand. When writing a biography for young readers, keep in mind that kids like to read about kids. Make sure that a good part of your story is devoted to the subject's childhood. Kids don't just want a recounting of the major events of a character's life. You should include anecdotal information about your subject's early life, too. If you are interested in writing biographies, take a look at the ones in your public library. Jean Fritz's very creative biographies for young readers are especially worth studying.
- **How-to/Activity books** teach readers a certain skill. Popular topics include cooking for children, magic, any child-oriented craft (like friendship bracelets, for instance), and science fair projects. These books are usually highly visual. They are illustrated either with black-and-white or color illustrations or with photographs. The instructions are usually in a step-by-step format, and any needed materials are listed separately. Safety issues—like using an oven only with parental supervision, for instance—are emphasized.
- **Science books** are an important category of nonfiction books. In looking for science topics, consider how these subjects relate to school curricula. In lower grades, dinosaurs, insects, habitats (ocean, prairie, etc.), fossils, simple machines, the weather and the human body are all typical curriculum topics. A nonfiction book relating to any one of these categories will likely be attractive to publishers. As our culture becomes more sensitive to the well-being of our planet, environmental topics will also become more and more popular.

• **Behind the scenes books** take many forms, but the most popular ones focus on an everyday object—a cookie, for example—and show the reader how that item was produced. These books usually include photographs taken at a factory site or acquired through a company's public relations department.
• **Holiday books** consider the origins, traditions and folklore of popular holidays. These books may also include "how-to" sections for crafts, games or holiday songs. Holiday books that discuss a holiday that is celebrated in school are especially popular.
• **History books** generally look at a single era or historical event, like the Civil Rights Movement, or they cover the history of a specific topic, such as ice skating.
• **Action books** consider an action-oriented sport, like drag racing, and convey the excitement and basic information of the sport through action-packed photographs and lively text.
• **Museum books** were popularized by the Eyewitness series, which uses concise and direct text to explain a particular subject. With high-interest, color photographs and artwork, the appeal of these books is primarily visual.

How Do I Know My Topic Will Sell?

One of the best ways to learn about the marketability of your nonfiction topic is to acquaint yourself with other books on the same or similar topics that are aimed at the same age level. You can do this by perusing the shelves at your library or, more systematically, by checking the subject index of *Books in Print*, a publication that lists every book in print by subject, author and title. Your library will have a copy of the most recent edition. You may also be able to access *Books in Print* through computer and modem.

If your topic is a popular one—dinosaurs, for instance—you'll need to consider carefully what unique approach or viewpoint will make your book stand out from the rest.

If there are few or no books about the topic you've selected, ask yourself whether the topic is truly one that will appeal to kids and to publishers of children's books. You'll also need to ask yourself if there is enough information, especially up-to-date information, about the topic.

When selecting your topic, consider its timeliness. Is it a topic that will interest today's kids? Also consider whether the material will become dated quickly. If your topic is tied to a current event—like the Olympics, the election or the appearance of a certain comet streaking through the sky—begin preparing your project at least two and a half years in advance and plan to contact a publisher two years before the event.

Also consider the scope of your project. Is your topic too broad for the proposed book format and intended audience? Can you cover it in a reasonable number of pages? By the same token, is it too narrow in scope? Would it be better as a magazine article, for instance, rather than an entire book?

More than anything else, make sure your topic can be approached in a way that is appealing to kids and is easy to understand. While some topics are more entertaining than others, be certain that you can have fun researching and writing about the topic. After all, you'll be writing for some time about this single subject. It should be a topic for which you can summon energy and enthusiasm.

How to Learn About Nonfiction Series

Many publishers that publish for libraries and schools, and some that publish for the bookstore market, have series of nonfiction titles. The themes for these series run the gamut—from biographies of famous female environmentalists to series of books on various addictive substances to books on habitats. You can get a sense of what these series are by visiting your library or bookstore. You can also write to individual publishers and request their catalog and writers' guidelines, which will show the range of series that they offer. (For more on how to approach publishers about guidelines and catalogs, see chapter six, pages 73-75.)

Then, if appropriate, you can pursue a topic that will fit perfectly within one of these already developed series. Is a series about girls' sports missing a book on rhythmic gymnastics? Is a series on addictive behaviors missing a book on gambling? Finding a topic that works within an already developed series means that your manuscript can more easily find a "place" on a publisher's list.

How to Come up With Cutting Edge Nonfiction Topics

- Talk to some teachers and learn the units of study that are offered at each grade level. If your state has a proficiency test, investigate the history and science topics covered.
- Read, clip and file information on children's leisure pursuits that might make good nonfiction topics—anything from sports to the arts.
- Make yourself aware of the activities in which young adults and older kids are involved. Remember that trends filter down. What is popular among teenagers will probably soon become popular with kids.
- Review children's magazines and note the topics of their nonfiction articles. (Again, children's magazines respond to trends in the marketplace much more quickly than book publishers, so their topics are more cutting edge. When you are looking at magazines for ideas, make sure you distinguish between an article on a kid-appealing nonfiction topic and one on a fad that will soon fade.)
- Consider issues that are in the news that will continue to affect kids and interest them. The environment, guns and drive-by shootings, natural disasters and child labor are just a few topics that might be refined for nonfiction books.

How do you determine whether your idea fits an existing series? A simple query letter will give you an answer. (We'll be discussing query letters in detail in chapter seven.)

The Elements of Nonfiction

While the breadth and depth of your topic, along with the level of your audience, will guide how you organize your book, most nonfiction books incorporate the same basic elements.

Your book's opener—which can be in the form of an opening chapter in a chapter book or a simple paragraph in a shorter book—should create a sense of awe about your topic so your reader will continue reading. It should also create a sense of urgency about the subject matter and communicate why the topic is worth knowing about.

There are several techniques you can use to pull the reader into your book. Anecdotes, "you are there" scenarios and amazing facts are just some of the ways you can grab your reader's attention. (For examples of effective openings, see the box on page 52.)

The body of a nonfiction book is organized according to the logic of the topic itself. Historical books and biographies should, generally, be organized chronologically. Books about science topics may be organized by kind of species or in some other sequential form. "How-to" books usually introduce simpler projects or skills before more complicated ones.

In determining your organization, remember that you must present your information in a way that a reader can understand sequentially—introducing simpler topics as a foundation for more complicated ones. And, if you are dealing with complicated topics, remember that young readers will absorb these ideas in "small chunks." It's best to use short paragraphs and short sentences and to introduce one fact at a time.

Another useful technique is to present difficult information in terms of a kid's world. Try to think of a way to compare the information you are presenting with something the reader can immediately visualize. Comparing a heart to the size of one's fist, for instance, is an easy way for children to grasp the size and shape of their own hearts. When you describe a time period, compare it to something a child knows well—a whole year in school, for instance, or the period of time between Easter and Christmas. First give the factual information and then back it up with a graphic explanation or an image that a child can understand.

You can also break up information by using headings and/or subheadings to allow the reader to easily browse through the material. The headings both introduce the reader to the next topic being discussed and show the reader (and the teacher or librarian), at a glance, what the book covers. The headings also allow readers to skip sections that they may not be interested in, which is especially helpful if they are preparing a report for school.

It's also helpful to break up your narrative with lists and timelines, charts and the like. You might also consider including special information that you want to highlight in boxes, similar to the boxed information in this book. Keep in mind that young readers are easily overwhelmed by large chunks of type. At the same time,

Openings That Will Grab Your Reader

ANECDOTAL

The evening is silent except for the rhythm of the cricket's song. Out of nowhere, a giant black glider soars from the darkening clouds toward the ground. There's a slight scratching sound followed by a tiny scream.

The barn owl, the fiercest hunter of the evening sky, has found its victim.

YOU ARE THERE

You feel the engine rattle beneath you. You hold tight to the trembling steering wheel. In front of you, the signal pole flashes its bright light. The engine beneath explodes in a sudden wave of power. You are the driver behind the wheel of one of the world's most powerful machines—the drag racer.

QUOTATION

"These waters foam pure white. Best keep your wits about you. And be ready to bail when I give the order." Those are the words of advice whitewater guide Jim Clemmons gives his crew before they take off down West Virginia's New River on board a flimsy rubber raft. Jim's crew will soon learn just how flimsy that raft is.

STATEMENT

Earth has not been here forever. Neither have the sun or moon, Mercury or Mars, or any of the other planets.

IMAGINE THIS

Imagine a strange underwater world, with turretted castles reaching toward the sun, tiny horses dancing next to colorful waving fans, and brilliant flashes of fish darting through the water.

Welcome to the incredible underwater world of the coral reef.

QUESTION

What is the Milky Way, anyway?

STATISTICS

The rain forest is home to more different species of plants and animals than any other habitat on earth. But this incredible habitat is dying. Every sixty seconds, an area of the rain forest the size of a football field is being destroyed.

though, don't go overboard. You don't want to run the risk of making your nonfiction book look too much like a textbook.

Most nonfiction books conclude with a glossary, a bibliography and an index. There may also be a list of books for further inquiry and a list of places to write for additional information on a topic. Teachers, parents and kids especially like lists of resources and government agencies that provide "free stuff"—pamphlets, information sheets, etc. You could also provide a list of ways the reader can become directly involved in the topic. If the book is about manatees, for instance, tell the reader how to help save these endangered creatures.

Opening Yourself up to Nonfiction

More than anything, you need to follow your dream as a writer, to write what you need and want to write. But it's just as important to stretch yourself by trying new genres. After you've tried writing nonfiction, you may find that it's just not for you, and you can return to that picture book or chapter book you're determined to write. On the other hand, you may find a new and creative endeavor in nonfiction, one that will lead you to rewarding publishing opportunities.

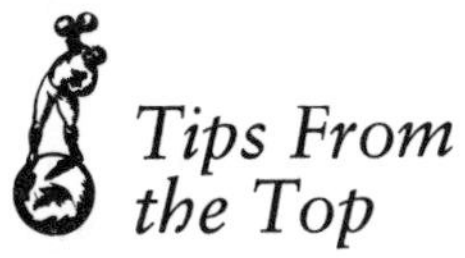

1. Make sure your research is solid and includes primary source material.

2. Keep a thorough list of your sources, including title, author, page numbers and copyright date.

3. Make sure that you are relying on the most up-to-date sources possible.

4. Be careful about paraphrasing your sources. When writing nonfiction, it can be tempting to paraphrase too closely and inadvertently plagiarize from your source.

5. Make sure that you have acquired permission from a source to use any diagrams, photographs or quotes of more than fifty words. Include the appropriate credit.

6. Verify your facts in at least three sources.

7. If you are writing about information that is technical, ask an expert in the field to review your manuscript before you submit it.

8. Be sure that you have identified the reasons your topic will be of interest to kids and to that particular publisher.

9. Make sure your topic and your writing style are appropriate for the age level of your audience.

10. Offer a unique twist on a tried and true topic. If you are proposing a book on dinosaurs, be clear about why your book will be different from all the others available.

11. If you can narrow your topic down enough, consider trying your idea out as a magazine article first. That will test the marketability of your topic and help you hone your writing style.

Inspiration Exercises

1. Read five nonfiction books written for the same age level on the same topic. If you need help, ask a librarian to recommend some favorites. Consider how each book treats its subject differently.

2. Look at those same books and study their openings. How did the authors grab the reader's attention? Were some of the openings better than others? Why?

3. Consider the following: the weight of a polar bear, the size of a hummingbird, the speed of a race car, the distance to the moon. Now think of ways that you can compare these measurements to things a child can visualize.

4. Play the game of "tens." Think of ten things that a kid likes in a certain category—ten foods, ten games, ten sports, ten animals, ten "famous" contemporary people, ten people from history. Consider how some of these items might be used as a topic for a nonfiction book, especially a "behind the scenes" book. Save the list for future reference.

5. Make a list of holidays that your family celebrates. Consider what you already do in terms of ritual, food, music, activities and crafts. Choose one aspect of the holiday and outline a nonfiction book about it.

6. Think about all the reasons why kids ask "why." Make a list and identify the ones that might make good nonfiction topics. And be sure to make a note the next time you hear a child ask "why" about something.

7. Consider ways you can deal with the transitions of a young child's life in a nonfiction format (beginning school, the birth of a sibling, starting a new sport, etc.).

8. Think of a skill you have that other people—especially kids—don't. This could be anything from gardening to a knowledge of sign language. Think about how you might turn that skill into a "how-to" activity book.

9. Research a famous historical figure and identify one or two episodes from that person's childhood that would appeal to young readers.

10. Choose a decade from history. From your own knowledge base or from a little research, write down ten things that happened during that era that kids might want to know about.

5 LOOK LIKE A PRO

You've probably heard the horror stories about the stacks and stacks of manuscripts that publishers receive each day from writers who have dreams of having their book published just like you do. Unfortunately, the horror stories are, for the most part, true. Publishers *do* receive large numbers of manuscripts each day, and they do reject most of them. That's a fact that all writers simply have to deal with.

But by learning some basic conventions of style, you can ensure that your manuscript receives serious consideration from a publisher. And, after all, it's serious consideration that may lead to serious publication.

Viewpoint

You can probably recall a story or book in which you felt as if you *became* the story's main character. You felt what the character felt and you experienced what the character experienced. In fact, you probably identified and empathized so completely with that character that you felt as if you had lived the entire story through the character's eyes.

You felt that way as a reader because the writer did an especially good job using a technique called single character viewpoint. And it's that quality and technique that an editor is most likely going to look for in your story.

Most stories for children are told through the viewpoint of the child who is the story's main character. That's because the story's reader needs to be most involved with that character emotionally.

How can you ensure that you have used single character viewpoint in your manuscript?

First of all, ask yourself: "Whose story is this?" When you ask yourself this question, you're not only trying to identify your main character. You've probably already done that. You're also considering how you can shape the events of the plot so the reader will fully identify with that character.

When you use single character viewpoint, you tell that character's story—and that character's story *only*. Every single thing in the plot—whether it's an event, problem, emotion or consequence—should be revealed through that main character's eyes. Your main character needs to be on center stage throughout the entire story, acting and reacting.

You need to reveal only your main character's emotions and thoughts. Tell your reader only what your main character is feeling, not the feelings of other characters.

You are probably thinking, "But surely I need to reveal the emotions, reactions and thoughts of the other important characters in the story." You're right, you do if they are important to the plot. You can do so by allowing your main character to observe those reactions for the reader.

Here's an example. This first passage demonstrates a viewpoint that is completely out of control. The writer has not used single character viewpoint and, therefore, the reader does not know who to identify with. The emotions of the other characters are revealed, but not through the main character's point of view.

> Jessica came bounding down the stairs with a smile on her face. She was going so fast that she practically ran into Jamie and Samantha.
>
> "Hey, where are you going in such a hurry?" Jamie asked, puzzled.
>
> Samantha was just as confused as Jamie was. "Yeah. What's up?" she asked impatiently.

Jessica's heart leapt as she shared the news. "Oh! I just got the best news. I'm going to be the lead in the musical."

"That's great," said Jamie, trying to summon up some enthusiasm. Deep down, she felt a stab of jealousy. She had wanted the part so badly, and now her best friend had gotten it. She tried to imagine what Jessica would look like on stage in the lead role, singing the song she was supposed to have sung.

Samantha tapped on Jessica's books impatiently. "How in the world are you going to work that into your schedule?" she asked. Samantha knew from experience that Jessica had trouble managing her time. She had cancelled their plans to study together twice in one week.

Jessica took a long look at her friends. Then she mentally reviewed her list of activities.

"I'll manage," she said, with a casual nod. "Just don't worry."

In this next passage, the writer has chosen Jessica as her main character and used single character viewpoint focused through Jessica's eyes. Jessica's emotions and reactions are revealed fully. The emotions and the reactions of the other characters are revealed as Jessica sees them.

Jessica was so excited that she practically flew down the stairs. She couldn't wait to tell her friends the news! She was going so fast that she almost ran right into Jamie and Samantha.

"Hey, where are you going in such a hurry?" Jamie asked.

"Yeah. What's up?" Samantha asked.

Jessica's heart leapt as she shared the news. "I just can't believe it. I'm going to be the lead in the musical."

"That's great," Jamie said.

Jessica thought she could hear a ring of jealousy in Jamie's voice. Jessica knew that she had been up for the role, too, but she'd thought that Jamie would at least be happy for her.

Samantha tapped on her books. "How in the world are you going to work that into your schedule?" Samantha asked.

Jessica thought about that one for a second. She had to admit she had been a bit overbooked lately. She had even had to change her plans to study with her friends. But acting in this play was more important than anything else she had ever done.

Jessica took a long look at her friends. "I'll manage," she said, with a casual nod.

She saw the doubtful looks on Samantha and Jamie's faces. "Just don't worry."

The changes are subtle, but important. They allow the reader to empathize with a single character in the story, rather than the entire cast.

Character Description

An editor is going to look for characters in your story that are realistic, believable and consistent throughout the entire book. Your main character, of course, should be your most developed and should also be the character who changes and grows most significantly from beginning to end.

One of the best ways to ensure that you are creating an effective main character is to spend some time really getting to know her. Some writers do this by writing a simple character sketch about their main character, detailing her likes and dislikes, her motivation, her goals, her age and personal history, and her physical qualities. (The character worksheet on page 61 guides you in writing a character sketch.)

Other writers find it easier to let their characters "talk" to them by writing a letter from their main character to themselves. Some writers prefer "interviewing" the main character as if she were actually in the same room. Other writers write a character statement in which the character speaks in first person about herself. These latter exercises have the advantage of actually establishing that character's voice. Whichever method you choose, you'll get to know your character more intimately. And, while you probably won't work into the story all of the character traits and details that you develop during this exercise, you'll know them, and this will help you maintain your character's consistency.

Secondary characters also need to be developed, although not as fully. If you're developing several secondary characters, be sure you can tell them apart. One way to do this is by developing "shorthand" traits for these characters. Perhaps one character loves cookies and is always eating. Maybe another is always chewing and popping her gum. Still another could love dolphins and always wear dolphin T-shirts or dolphin jewelry. Of course, you'll need to develop these characters in a bit more detail than this, but such shorthand traits can help your reader immediately identify the character at hand.

Whatever you do, be consistent in terms of characterization and physical description. A character who has short brown hair on page 7 can't suddenly have long blonde hair on page 44. A character who has just had his thirteenth birthday on page 9 can't be able to drive on page 90. Such mistakes sound absurd, but they are easy to make if you're not careful, especially when dealing with the minor characters you may not know as well as your major ones.

Character Development

An editor will also be looking for substantial character growth on the part of the main character. That means that the main character can't be *too* perfect at a story's outset. One of the biggest complaints that editors have about characters is that they are "too good to be believed." Your character should be likable, but the character shouldn't react so honorably that he seems phony or contrived.

When character growth does occur in a story, editors will look to see whether you have *shown* the reader the process of that character growth. Were you clear about what has caused the character to change? It's not enough for a character to suddenly decide to do the right thing. An event in the plot needs to compel her to change. Show the reader the reasoning process she goes through as she decides to make that change.

CHARACTER WORKSHEET

Name: ____________________

Physical characteristics

age and grade level: ____________________

hair color: ____________________

eye color: ____________________

size: ____________________

build: ____________________

other physical traits: ____________________

Personality traits: ____________________

____

Environmental factors (bedroom, home, school, town): ____________________

____

____

Likes/dislikes: ____________________

____

____

Other characters and how the main character feels about them: ____________________

____

____

What motivates this character? ____________________

____

____

How does this character grow and change from beginning to end? ____________________

____

____

Write a note from this character in first person: ____________________

____

____

Stereotypes

Editors—and young readers—react negatively to characters that are stereotypes. You will probably find it easy to identify racial or gender-based stereotypes in your story, but you might not recognize the more subtle ones. Consider these:

- The friendly grandmother, who wears a bright apron, always smells of cookies, and is ready to lend advice at a moment's notice.
- The grouchy old man at the end of the street who softens when a child character performs some friendly act.
- The class bully who is always ready to pick a fight.
- The poor little rich girl who has all the material things she wants but no friends.

There's nothing wrong with using one of these stereotypes as a jumping off point for a character, but editors will look for characters with a little more depth. They are looking for writers who are creative enough to go beyond these traditional—but tired—characters.

Dialogue

Handling dialogue effectively is one of the real signs of an accomplished writer. That means not only handling it correctly in terms of punctuation and indentation, but using it appropriately in your story.

Let's consider the fine points of punctuation and paragraphing first.

When a character speaks—and only when he speaks out loud, as opposed to speaking to himself in a kind of internal dialogue—put his words between two sets of quotation marks. The punctuation that ends his statement goes inside those quotation marks.

If you are following his statement with a tag line, such as "he said" or "she said," a comma precedes the quotation mark *unless* his statement is a question or an exclamation. In those cases, a question mark or an exclamation point is used; and it goes inside the quotation marks as well. Examine the following examples of punctuation in dialogue.

I really want to go, Sally begged silently.

"I am going," Sally said.

Sally said, "I am going."

"Can I go?" Sally asked.

"I am going!" Sally said.

Now let's consider a longer passage of dialogue, one that continues after the tag line. If the dialogue is all one sentence, a comma should be placed after the tag line, before the continuation of the sentence:

"I am going," Sally said, "whether you give me permission or not."

If, on the other hand, the continuation of the dialogue is really a separate sentence, place a period after the tag line and begin a new sentence with quotation marks, like this:

"I am going," Sally said. "That's final."

There's a second essential rule of dialogue: Every time a different character speaks, begin a new paragraph. If you are including a conversation in your story, you will need a good number of paragraph breaks within that conversation—every time someone different begins to talk.

Here are a few other fine points of dialogue to help you look like a pro.

• Don't try too hard to vary your tag lines. "He said" and "she said" are accepted and sound natural. Some beginning writers carry their tag lines so far they almost sound comical: "she questioned," "he exclaimed," "she hissed," "he insisted." Vary them occasionally where it feels appropriate, but don't try to change them every time.

• When you do choose to vary your tag lines, do so with verbs that actually describe speech. People don't laugh or giggle at the same time as they talk. Those are separate activities. A phrase like

" 'That was a great joke,' she laughed," should be changed to " 'That was a great joke,' she said with a laugh."

• Don't overuse adjectives to describe the tenor of the dialogue. Again, beginning writers sometimes go overboard, qualifying every single tag line: he said joyously, she said sadly, he said gaily, she said morosely. If you feel you need adjectives like this to qualify your dialogue, use them occasionally for effect. Better yet, allow the character's speech to convey the emotion you intend.

Word Choice

While you don't need to worry too much about word choice, you do need to read your manuscript carefully, looking for words that seem stilted or stiff or that are completely beyond the comprehension of the reader. *Therefore* and *however* are two words that rarely belong in children's books.

More important than the complexity of the word you've chosen is the specific meaning of the word, especially in description. The best way to create effective "word pictures" is to use specific and concrete language, words that really say what you mean. When crafting your story, consider some of the more general adjectives or word choices you've made. Have you described something as "beautiful," "colorful," or "nice"? Instead, find a way to let your reader know *how* something is beautiful. What colors make the object colorful? How is someone nice? These are words that we use all the time, so often that they have come to have general meanings. As a writer, your job is to find not only the right word to describe something, but the best, most precise word.

Sentence Structure

Editors are looking for writing that is understandable, but lively. Use a variety of different kinds of sentences. When worrying about readability and reading level, it's easy to fall into the trap of using short, simple, declarative sentences. Fight that tendency. Vary your sentence structure and your writing will be more interesting.

Most good writing is written in active voice. As you review your work, recast as many passive sentences as you can in active voice. Passive voice describes action that is performed *by* a character.

Active voice puts the character first and describes the character actually doing the activity. Here is an example to demonstrate the difference:

> (Passive voice) The baseball glove and mitt were held out by Brian like a peace offering.
>
> (Active voice) Brian held out the baseball glove and mitt like a peace offering.

Watch for two common problems: sentence fragments and run-on sentences. It's OK to use sentence fragments occasionally and deliberately for effect, but don't overuse them. Take a careful look at some of your longer sentences and see if they can be broken into two—or even three—sentences. While you might join two sentences of similar meaning with a semicolon when writing for adult readers, avoid that punctuation mark when you write for younger readers.

Tense Changes

Beginning writers sometimes make the mistake of mixing present tense with past tense in a single story. While present tense creates a sense of immediacy in your story, it is a deceptively difficult technique to use. Past tense simply sounds more natural and is more conventional. Most importantly, be sure that you have used past tense consistently throughout your story or piece.

The Final Proofing Process: How Not to Embarrass Yourself

I was once in the middle of an interview for an editorial position I really wanted when the interviewer was called away for a few minutes. After she left, I glanced over my cover letter and resumé that she had left behind on her desk.

Suddenly, I noticed a glaring error. The word *Ohio*, my home state, was spelled "Oho." While I don't know whether she noted the error, I was so embarrassed by the mistake that I was worthless for the rest of the interview.

I didn't get the job, but the experience taught me three valuable lessons.

First of all, it is often the most obvious mistake that is missed.

Second of all, computer spellcheckers lull us into a false sense of security (it had passed by *Oho*).

Lastly, it's always a good idea—no matter how good a proofreader you are or how many times you've proofed your story—to run your final draft by someone else.

There are a few other proofreading tips that will make your manuscript look professionally polished:

- Double-check passages that have been substantially rewritten to ensure that you haven't introduced additional mistakes.
- Make sure you have handled words with variant spellings consistently. If you choose to use *dived* instead of *dove*, or *t-shirt* instead of *T-shirt*, make sure that you use it the same way throughout the entire story. (You'll find it helpful to keep a list of tricky words like these so you can double-check yourself accurately.)
- Double-check the spelling of the characters' names and make sure that you have spelled them correctly and consistently. You'll find this easier to do if you use standard names and standard spellings.
- Carefully check any technical terms, place names, names of "real" people (how easy it would be to misspell *Einstein*), and dates and numbers (look to make sure you haven't transposed numbers or simply used the wrong number). Make sure you check the big things as well as the small. Look at your title, your name, your address, your chapter names, and so on.
- Look at your punctuation. Make sure you haven't put a comma where a period should be and vice versa.
- Read your manuscript aloud one last time. Then, if it isn't too long, try what the real pros do: Read it backwards, to yourself or out loud. You'll look at your work in a different way and you may spot a glaring error.

Being Confident

If you've written a children's story or book-length manuscript that you are excited about, you should feel enthusiastic about your

Some Matters of Style

• Capitalize *mom*, *dad*, *grandma*, etc., when used in place of a proper name. When used with a modifier, use lowercase letters.

When I asked Mom if I could go, she said no.

When I asked my mom if I could go, she said no.

• When punctuating dialogue, the end punctuation goes inside the quotation marks.

"Mom, can I go?" she asked.

"Mom, I want to go," she said.

• Do not use quotation marks when a character is using inner dialogue or thinking in segments that sound like dialogue. Some style guides suggest that you underline or italicize these. Others prefer that they are handled with no special treatment. Either of these is correct:

She just has to let me go, I begged silently.

It's not fair. Everyone else gets to go, I thought.

She just has to let me go, I begged silently.

It's not fair. Everyone else gets to go, I thought.

• Begin a new paragraph every time a different character speaks or uses inner dialogue.

"But I really want a dog," Jamie begged.
"We've talked about this, Jamie," his mom answered. "We just don't have the room."
"And where would we take it for a walk?" his sister Emily asked.
"Besides, you have two lizards, five fish, and three birds already," his father said.
I've got to change their minds, Jamie thought to himself. *There's got to be a way!*

• An "em dash" is used to set off a phrase for emphasis. In dialogue, an em dash indicates an abrupt change in the thought process or interruption of speech. Em dashes are indicated by two dashed lines. Some computers provide an extended hyphen as an em dash.

> There were lots of kids going—practically the whole third grade—but not me.
> "Please let me go. If you just say yes, I'll—"
> "You'll what?" Mom interrupted.

• Ellipses are used to show a trailing off in speech or a pause in speech.

> "Please let me. . . ." Oh, what was the use. She'd never let me go.

• A hyphen (a single dash) is used to hyphenate words. (Avoid hyphens altogether in picture books and early readers.)

> Phillip was a six-year-old boy who just hated first grade.

> April had found herself in the ultimate no-win situation.

• Don't overuse capitalization. Seasons aren't capitalized, nor are most general locations. Consult a good, unabridged dictionary when you have questions. When in doubt, leave it lowercase.

> (Incorrect) It was a lovely Spring day. Becca rode her bike to the Town Square. She leaned her bike against the gazebo and headed to the Ice Cream Store.

> (Correct) It was a lovely spring day. Becca rode her bike to the town square. She leaned her bike against the gazebo and headed into Morgan's Ice Cream Shop.

• An apostrophe indicates the possessive form of a noun. Don't be careless about the way you use it. Sometimes, beginning writers mistakenly use apostrophes to indicate plural nouns.

(Incorrect) All of the moms' and dads' were there.

(Correct) All of the moms and dads were there.

- Learn the commonly used (and misused) homonyms and make sure you use them correctly.

their (possessive form of *they*/**there** (a pronoun for a location)
its (possessive form of *it*)/**it's** (contraction for *it is*)
whose (possessive form of *who*)/**who's** (contraction for *who is*)

- Weed out dated references.

characters who smoke pipes
make-up in compacts
vanity instead of *dressers*
davenport instead of *couch*
pocketbook instead of *purse*

- Watch for overused punctuation. Exclamation points and commas are frequently overused by beginning writers.

(Incorrect) She couldn't believe it! She was actually going to play goalie! She couldn't wait to tell her mom the news! She would be so proud of her!

One well-placed exclamation point is really more effective:

(Correct) She couldn't believe it! She was actually going to play goalie. She couldn't wait to tell her mom the news. Her mom would be so proud of her.

work. Don't let yourself get carried away with that enthusiasm, though. Remember, it's not just the story that the editor will be considering. She'll also be looking to see that you know the accepted conventions of children's literature and good fiction, and she'll expect a manuscript that has been thoroughly revised and proofread.

Don't sabotage yourself by submitting work that looks amateurish. Take some time with your manuscript, allow it to rest, then make sure you revise it thoroughly. But revision isn't enough. Let your manuscript rest again, and then proofread it several times. After you've finished, ask someone else to proofread it as well.

When you finally put that manuscript in an envelope and walk it to the post office, you'll be confident that you are submitting a manuscript that is as professional as you can make it. That is the best way to make sure your manuscript will be met with professional consideration.

Tips From the Top

1. Make sure that you have thoroughly proofread your manuscript before you submit it to a publisher. (Consider enlisting the help of a professional to ensure accuracy.) Make necessary corrections, and then have the manuscript retyped. Do not submit manuscripts with handwritten corrections.

2. Use single character viewpoint: Tell your story through the viewpoint of the main character in the story.

3. Avoid addressing the reader directly, using such phrases as "Do you know what happened next?" These references not only sound dated and patronizing, they probably indicate places where you have stepped out of the viewpoint.

4. Make sure that your characters are believable kids. They shouldn't be all good or all bad. They should react as real children do.

5. Show the way your character undergoes change. Avoid plots in which the character suddenly comes to realize that he or she needs to pursue a new direction.

6. Learn the basic conventions of spelling, grammar and punctuation, and apply them.

7. Consult an unabridged dictionary for questions about spelling and capitalization.

8. Learn to second-guess your word processor's spell-check program. Double-check homonyms or other words that you might consistently misuse.

Inspiration Exercises

1. Select several books of fiction (both picture books and books for older readers) from your personal or public library shelves. See how long it takes to determine through whose viewpoint the story is told. Then see if you can identify the ways the author established that viewpoint.

2. Choose a character from one of your favorite books or fairy tales. Use the character worksheet to identify various traits about the character. If these traits aren't mentioned in the author's story, see if you can speculate about what they might be. When you are finished, consider the ways the author used character description and character growth to enhance the story.

3. Consider the following descriptive words: *handsome*, *red*, *happy*, *funny*. Come up with three descriptive words for each of these that are more specific than the one mentioned.

4. Think of several stereotypical characters. Consider ways you might make these characters more dimensional. What different take could you offer on the friendly grandmother? What new traits could you give the class clown?

5. Study closely passages of dialogue in children's books and adult novels. Look at how the passages are punctuated and where paragraphs are introduced. Consider how often the speaker is identified. Study what verbs are used in the dialogue's tag lines.

6 FIND THE RIGHT PUBLISHER FOR YOUR BOOK

You've revised your manuscript until you can't revise it any more. You've tested it out on a group of kids or presented it to your own writing group. You've fine-tuned, tightened and streamlined. You've proofed it, proofed it again and asked a friend to proofread it for you. You're confident that it is ready to be published.

Now how do you find a publisher? And, more importantly, how do you find the *right* publisher for your book?

How to Find the Appropriate Publisher

You may have heard fellow writers or editors say that the publishing game is a "crap shoot." You need luck on your side if you want to attract an editor's attention.

Finding the right publisher for your book has more to do with accurate and effective research than with luck. There are lots and lots of publishers, but they don't all publish the same thing. Many publishers specialize in particular kinds of children's books. They may publish more books in a specific category than in another. They may not publish in specific genres—like fantasy or poetry. They may consider certain subjects taboo. Even if they don't specialize, some publishers may be looking for a book with a particular tone or type of character.

How do you find out what publishers are publishing? Here are some terrific tools to help you find your way through the publishing maze.

Market Guides

There are several market guides that provide information about what kinds of manuscripts specific publishers look for. The most comprehensive of these is *Children's Writer's and Illustrator's Market*, which provides a listing of every publisher, both magazine and book, and what kind of work they publish. This guide also provides detailed information on the market for children's books and magazine articles, and includes articles about the state of the business and interviews with editors and authors. *The Children's Writer Guide* published by Children's Writer newsletter is also a valuable resource for information about publishers, as well as trends, interviews with authors and editors, and assessments of the industry as a whole. *The Christian Writers' Market Guide* is a great resource for information about Christian magazine and book publishers.

These guides are updated every year and you should consult the most recent guide available, since publishers' needs change frequently. You should not rely on these guides exclusively, however. Make sure you back up the information you find there with information from other sources.

Writer's Guidelines

Most publishers provide guidelines that spell out their various needs. At the most basic level, the guidelines should tell you whether the publisher is accepting unsolicited and/or unagented manuscripts at that time. (An unsolicited manuscript is a manuscript that the editor hasn't formally requested from an author.) If they aren't accepting unagented material, there's no point in sending them your manuscript. If they are not accepting unsolicited manuscripts, you can still reach them by sending a query letter describing your manuscript and credentials, rather than the entire manuscript. (For more on query letters, see pages 82-84.)

Many writer's guidelines are specific about subject matter, word length, approach and submission procedure. The guidelines might also tell you about new series or book lines.

To get writer's guidelines, you simply need to send a letter of request. The letter should be simple and direct, and contain a self-addressed stamped envelope (SASE) for the return of the guidelines.

SAMPLE LETTER REQUESTING WRITER'S GUIDELINES

Jennifer Raffin
1722 Eagle Nest's Row
Spinsville, Nevada XXXXX

Date

Leapfrog Press
16666 Lemon Lane
Expresstown, New Mexico 33333

Dear Sir or Madam,

I am writing to request your writer's guidelines. I have enclosed a SASE for your convenience.

Thank you. I'll look forward to hearing from you.

Sincerely,

Jennifer Raffin

Catalogs

You can also get an idea of what publishers are publishing by reviewing their current catalogs. Catalogs can be especially helpful to flesh out information about existing book series, as well as the age categories the publishers are targeting. Often, too, you can get a feel for the publishers' tastes from their catalog designs.

These catalogs are also available to you. Simply include a request for these along with your request for guidelines. (Some publishers may charge a nominal fee for a catalog. Even if they don't, be sure to include enough postage for return of the catalog.) Bookstores and libraries order primarily through catalogs, so if you work or have friends in that industry, you may have access to them through those connections.

Newsletters and Magazines

Magazines targeted to writers, like *Writer's Digest* or *The Writer*, often contain market guide sections with information about an editor's immediate needs. Publishing industry magazines, such as *Publishers Weekly* mentioned in chapter one, occasionally have articles on new developments in children's book publishing. Several newsletters also provide up-to-the-minute information on publishers' needs: *Children's Writer*, the *SCBWI Bulletin* and the *Children's Book Insider* are three excellent resources worth the cost of the subscription. (You'll find addresses for these in the appendix on pages 116-117.)

The Books Themselves

Your research into publishers should also include a hard look at the books themselves. Often the publisher's writer's guidelines or the *Children's Writer's and Illustrator's Market* will suggest representative titles that best reflect the company's philosophy and publishing strategy.

Review a good number of the recent titles that the publisher has produced. Can you see your book manuscript fitting in with these books? Does your manuscript fit their overall approach? Is your book *too* similar to something they just produced? Would your book fit into one of their existing series?

Literary Marketplace

The *Literary Marketplace* is a comprehensive guide to all the companies that serve the publishing industry. The book is basically a sourcebook for addresses and phone numbers of publishers, packagers, printers, agents, and the like. While very little hard market data is included, this guide does provide names and addresses of editors and agents. It's quite expensive and probably not worth purchasing on its own. Most libraries carry it in their reference department.

Writers Conferences

Most communities have writers conferences that may feature an editor, an agent or another writer as a speaker. Often, these speakers will speak about the needs of particular publishers as the focus of their talk or during a question-and-answer session that follows. The conferences may also offer opportunities to meet an editor personally or to have a manuscript critiqued by an editor. Most writers find these experiences invaluable.

SCBWI (Society of Children's Book Writers and Illustrators) sponsors regional conferences throughout the country and a larger conference every summer in California. You can not only gain valuable market information at these conferences, but you can also develop friendships with other writers. For a list of conferences, consult *Children's Writer's and Illustrator's Market*.

Industry Gossip

You may have a source of market news right under your nose. Publishers' sales representatives often have inside information about what types of books their publisher is pursuing. Other children's writers in your community may also have some information from their contacts. You can usually depend on librarians and bookstore owners to have a handle on what publishers are publishing. Don't be afraid to ask those friends, friends of friends, and colleagues who may have a connection to publishing. Then double-check the accuracy and timeliness of their information with the market guides, publishers' guidelines or newsletters mentioned above.

Matching Your Manuscript to the Right Publisher

In your research, you will probably find three or four publishers that are likely candidates for publishing your story. How do you decide which one to approach?

How to Research Publishers

1 Look through a market guide, such as *Children's Writer's and Illustrator's Market*. Read carefully the market data provided for each publisher that interests you. Make notes on the publishers who might be receptive to the manuscript you've written.

2 Using the address listings in the market guide, write to the publishers you've chosen and ask for writer's guidelines. These will tell you the overall philosophy of the company, the different book lines and the appropriate subject matter for those lines, length specifications, any readability standards, and possibly new directions the publisher is pursuing. Don't forget to include an SASE (self-addressed stamped envelope). You may also want to request a publisher's catalog at the same time. Include additional postage for the catalog.

3 While you are waiting for the guidelines, go to the library or your bookstore and study some of the books published by the publishers you've selected. Pay particular attention to books that have the same audience as your manuscript.

4 Next, look for at least one other source of information about the publishing companies you've selected. Try publications that carry reviews of recently published children's books—*Publishers Weekly*, *School Library Journal*, *American Bookseller*, *The Horn Book*. Scan the *SCBWI Bulletin*, *Writer's Digest*, or other newsletters and periodicals aimed at writers. If you have access to the Internet, visit a web site that features market information about children's book publishing. (For a list of such sites, see pages 117-118.)

5 If you have another source of information, use it to back up what you've found. This source may be an editor you met at a writers conference, a fellow writer, a teacher, librarian or publisher's sales representative. ✵

First of all, look carefully at the data you've gathered. Is there one publisher that matches your story's approach and subject matter very closely? Is that publisher currently looking for and accepting manuscripts? If the answer to both of these questions is yes, then you should approach that publisher first.

You can also choose to follow your heart—to approach the publisher that publishes books you *admire* the most. Make sure your manuscript fits reasonably within their needs and confirm that they are currently accepting manuscripts.

You should also consider the size of the publisher. Small publishing companies, especially newer companies just getting started, are sometimes more likely to take a chance on a manuscript from an unpublished writer. You will need to do a little bit of digging to determine whether the company is really a small company or simply an "imprint" of a larger company. (An imprint is a distinct line of books, a specialized interest within a larger publishing house.) Check *Literary Marketplace* to determine whether the company is on its own or an imprint.

Finally, you might also consider approaching an editor who recently has been hired at a particular publishing company. Newly hired editors are often looking to build their lists and will consider the work of unpublished authors. Sometimes the *SCBWI Bulletin* or *Publishers Weekly* has information on editors who have recently joined a publishing house. (For more on how to find out about editors, see chapter seven.)

Multiple Submissions: Approaching More Than One Publisher

What if you can't narrow down your choice to a single publisher? You can choose to submit the manuscript to several publishers at once. A manuscript submitted to more than one publisher at a time is called a multiple, or simultaneous, submission. Not so long ago, multiple submissions were considered bad form. A writer was expected to send her manuscript to one publisher, wait for a rejection, and then send it to another publisher. Because some publishers hold manuscripts as long as six months, writers lost a great deal of time in the submission process.

Today, some publishers have changed their policies and attitudes, but many still state in their guidelines that they do not accept multiple submissions. Others say they will accept them, but ask that you inform them that you are submitting it elsewhere at the same time. SCBWI has suggested its own policy—submit to one publisher at a time and allow them the exclusive right of review for two months. Then, if you don't hear from the publisher in two

Checklist for Targeting Publishers

- Does your manuscript fit the publisher's commercial and literary philosophy?
- Does your manuscript fit into a line of books the publisher is already producing?
- Is your manuscript too similar to something the publisher has just published?
- Is the subject matter taboo to the publisher for any reason? (Some religious publishers might object to a book about Halloween, for instance.)
- Does the manuscript match the publisher's particular niche in terms of age level and subject matter?
- Is the style of the manuscript in line with the publisher's needs and with the other books the publisher is publishing?
- Does the length of the manuscript match the publisher's guidelines? ✷

months time, write and tell them that you are withdrawing the manuscript from consideration, and then submit it elsewhere. As a matter of policy, SCBWI does *not* recommend multiple submissions.

Many writers simply ignore all policies. They select several publishers and make multiple submissions, without informing those publishers of the fact. What is the downside? Several exist. There is a possibility all the publishers will call on the same day and start a bidding war for the manuscript—a highly unlikely scenario especially for a first time author. Some writers express worry that two editors from different publishing houses might discover over a literary lunch that they have received the same manuscript at the same time. Again, this is a highly unlikely scenario. In truth, it's not terribly risky to ignore publishers' warnings about multiple submissions. As a writer, you need to make your own decision about the ethical implications of multiple submissions versus the practical considerations.

If you choose to make multiple submissions, don't blindly submit your manuscript to every publisher. Select the three to five publishers that are the most likely candidates and submit to them first. If you are rejected by all of them, select several more, and so on.

Here's one important caution: If you are submitting to more than one publisher, make sure the right manuscript goes in the right envelope. When I was an editor I sometimes received envelopes addressed to me, with cover letters and manuscripts addressed to another editor at another publishing company.

Market Research—Why Bother?

After all the work you've put into writing, revising and polishing your story, you may find the additional work of researching publishers daunting. You may even feel the research tasks are more involved than the writing! If you're feeling overwhelmed, keep in mind this simple rule of thumb: Find out as much as you can about various publishing companies from as many sources as you can. And then make a thoughtful and considered choice.

Researching publishers *is* an essential part of seeking publication. Selecting appropriate publishers will save you time—and will allow you to get back to the creative task of writing something new. But don't let the task overwhelm or intimidate you. And most importantly, don't let it stop you from taking the all-important step of submitting your work for publication!

Tips From the Top

1. Do thorough market research. Find out as much as you can about the publisher you want to approach from as many sources as you have available.

2. Find a way to systematize the information you receive. Keep files on each publisher, with guidelines, catalogs and other market tidbits. Organize your information in a notebook or on your computer. Don't spend too much time filing, but find a way to access the information quickly.

3. When visiting bookstores and libraries, train yourself to look for publishers as frequently as you do authors or titles.

4. Make sure you write for guidelines from publishers on a regular basis—every year or so. Publishers' needs change and they update their guidelines to reflect those changes. Some publishers post their guidelines on a web page.

5. Develop a network of writers who are also doing market research and submitting their work. (This is something that can be done through chat rooms on the Internet.) Discuss your analysis of various publishers' needs, your experience with specific publishers, and so on.

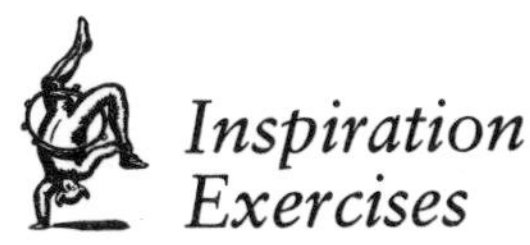

Inspiration Exercises

1. Choose one large publisher and one smaller, specialized publisher (a Christian publisher, for example). Read their descriptions in *Children's Writer's and Illustrator's Market.* Write to them requesting their guidelines. Find at least one other source of information about the publisher such as a catalog or an article in *Publishers Weekly* or *SCBWI Bulletin.* Then, brainstorm three or four ideas for each publisher.

2. Put yourself in the role of the publisher. Pick an existing piece of your work and create a set of writer's guidelines that exactly matches your work.

3. Think about your circle of friends, colleagues or acquaintances. Do any of them have contacts in the publishing world? Find a way to explore this further.

7 GIVE YOUR MANUSCRIPT A FIGHTING CHANCE

Your manuscript is ready, your research is done and it's time to take the most important step toward publishing your book—submitting it to a publisher.

How do you do it?

While there's no magic formula, there is one important rule of thumb: Make sure your submission is professional. Children's book editors are incredibly busy people. They have schedules that are full of meetings and conferences, most of which have nothing directly to do with discovering a terrific manuscript to publish. They need to use the little time they do have for reviewing manuscripts efficiently and carefully. You can make their job easier—and increase your chances of publishing with them—by preparing your manuscript package neatly and professionally.

You may have already spent time and energy worrying about just what to send publishers. Some writers spend so much time pondering this question they never get around to sending the manuscript at all. Here are some general guidelines to help you determine what is appropriate to submit.

Query Letters

A query letter describes your project and your credentials and asks an editor if she would like to see the rest of the manuscript. If you've written for magazines, especially adult magazines, then you know an engaging query letter is usually an essential part of the submission process.

In children's book publishing, the query letter is used less often. Send a query letter in these cases:

- When the publisher's guidelines specify that they prefer query letters.
- When publishers are not accepting unsolicited manuscripts.
- For nonfiction topics.
- For nonfiction series.

Note that that the tone and the content are straightforward and direct. If you write for magazines, you probably spend a lot of time making sure your query letters sound as jazzy as possible. This isn't necessary in children's book publishing—the editor is more interested in your book idea.

Keep in mind that if you have received a positive response to a query letter, you have not sold the publisher the book. They are simply willing to look at your manuscript.

Proposals

Proposals generally take the form of three sample chapters (usually the first three chapters), typed in manuscript form, a chapter-by-chapter outline and a cover letter. A proposal allows an editor to see at a glance whether the manuscript is appropriate for her list. Send a proposal in the following circumstances:

- When the publisher's guidelines specify that they prefer proposals.
- When a publisher has requested a proposal after being prompted by a query letter.
- For longer nonfiction books.
- For novels, especially middle grade novels.

Here it's important to refer directly to the writer's guidelines. They may prefer to see full manuscripts for middle grade novels, for example, and proposals for nonfiction books.

SAMPLE QUERY LETTER

Elizabeth Summer
42 Drew Boulevard
Benjamin, Arkansas XXXXX

Date

Josephine Darby
Rooster Publishing
XXXX 34th Street
New York, New York XXXXX

Dear Ms. Darby,

Underneath the shimmering waters of the shallow seas, an underwater world waits to be explored. *A Look Around Coral Reefs*, a nonfiction picture book, takes young readers (ages 5-8) to this habitat to explore the amazing plants and animals that live there. In easy-to-understand language, the book also explains camouflage, the food chain and symbiosis. Several sidebars contain "fun facts" about undersea life. A glossary and an index complete the manuscript. The manuscript runs about 1,300 words.

As a kindergarten teacher, I know that underwater habitats are one of the most popular of our curricular units. As an avid scuba diver, I have firsthand knowledge of the coral reef and the excitement it offers.

May I send you the completed manuscript for your review? Should you decide to contract the manuscript, I would be happy to provide underwater photographs to accompany the text. Please let me know if you would like me to include samples of these with the manuscript.

I am excited about the opportunity to introduce children to this unique underwater environment and to add my name to the fine list of authors at Rooster Publishing. I'll look forward to hearing from you.

Sincerely,

Elizabeth Summer
Enc: SASE

Elements of a Proposal

- Cover letter
- Biography
- Book synopsis
- Character sketches
- Chapter-by-chapter outline
- Three sample chapters
- Self-addressed stamped envelope
- Reply card—optional

Full Manuscript Package

A full manuscript package includes a manuscript typed in correct manuscript form. The package should also have a cover letter that describes the project, explains why the publisher should consider publishing it, and details the writer's credentials. It's appropriate to send a full manuscript:

- When the publisher's guidelines specify that they prefer full manuscripts. (If they accept either manuscripts or proposals, and you have completed and are confident about your manuscript, send the entire work.)
- For picture books and short chapter books.
- For shorter nonfiction books.

Besides the cover letter and manuscript, there is another essential ingredient to a manuscript package: an SASE (self-addressed, stamped envelope) for return of the manuscript should it be rejected. (For instructions on preparing an SASE, see page 86.) Some writers also include a self-addressed, stamped postcard and request that the editor mail it when the manuscript is received. With the return of the postcard, the author knows that the package has actually reached the editor and can gauge how long to wait for a response.

How to Prepare Your Manuscript

Your manuscript should be typed in black using a standard, easy-to-read font. Don't be tempted to use a decorative font, several different fonts or a color besides black. Your goal is to show off your manuscript, not the technology of your computer. The type should be all the same size as well. There is no need to type your

What Is an SASE Anyway?

The abbreviation SASE stands for self-addressed, stamped envelope. You include an SASE for the publisher's convenience so they can return your manuscript or send you guidelines, catalogs or other information.

To prepare a self-addressed, stamped envelope, first make sure your envelope is big enough to accommodate the manuscript or material you are requesting. Then type or write your name in both the address position and the return address position.

Prepare the envelope to the publisher at the same time. This time, put your address in the return address space only. Put the publisher's information in the address position.

Then take the entire package to the post office. Ask them to weigh the manuscript, with the SASE folded on top. Buy the appropriate postage twice—once for the manuscript and once for the SASE. Affix the appropriate postage to the SASE. Fold the SASE and put it, along with the manuscript, into the envelope addressed to the publisher. Then affix the same amount of postage to the publisher's envelope.

Now mail it!

name or your title in a larger type than the rest of the manuscript.

Dot matrix is acceptable, but it is often difficult to read. If your printer is dot matrix, make sure you use a new ribbon or ink cartridge to ensure the printed copy is dark enough.

Format for Picture Book Manuscripts or Books Without Chapters

Start by leaving good margins—at least an inch on each side and about an inch and a half at the bottom. At the top of your first page in the left-hand corner, type your name and address, telephone number, and social security number (this is optional). This text should be single spaced. In the right-hand corner, type the approximate number of words in the manuscript. (Some word processing programs will calculate the word count exactly. However, there's no need to be completely accurate when it comes to the word count. Figure 250 words per page and calculate it from there.)

Center your story's title about midway down the page, followed by your name. Then begin typing the story itself, double spaced, on the same page. Although this is page one of your manuscript, do not type a page number on this first page.

Type the rest of the manuscript starting at the top of the page, being sure to leave a one-inch margin. Number the rest of your manuscript consecutively at the top of the page. On each page, include the book's title as a heading next to the page number. (For an example of manuscript form for a picture book or a book without chapters, see pages 88-89.

Format for Chapter Books or Novels

If you are submitting an entire chapter book or novel, create a title page for the entire book. Type your name, address, phone number and social security number at the top left-hand corner as explained for the picture book manuscripts; again, this should be single-spaced. Then type your title in all caps about midway down the page. Include a byline a few lines beneath the title.

Begin typing the first chapter about midway down the next page (page two), placing the chapter title in the center. Begin a new page for each chapter, centering your title about midway down the page.

Again, consecutively number the manuscript starting with the first page of your first chapter. Include the chapter title as part of your heading.

You can also prepare a table of contents if you like, but it's not necessary. If you do so, include your table of contents before the first page of the first chapter.

Most editors prefer that you do not bind or staple your manuscript in any way. You may put a rubber band or a large paper clip around the entire work if you like, but even that is not necessary. For an example of manuscript form for a chapter book or novel, see pages 90-91.

Two final reminders: As tempting as it is, do not add a copyright notice to your title page. As we discussed in chapter one, your work is protected by copyright laws even without such a notice. And don't send along illustrations or illustration suggestions.

SAMPLE OF MANUSCRIPT FORM—PICTURE BOOK OR BOOK WITHOUT CHAPTERS

Emily Herrold
445 Maple Street
Bedford, Alabama XXXXX
social security number or date of birth

350 words

THE SUNSHINE MAN
By Emily Herrold

This is what your fiction or nonfiction book manuscript should look like when you send it off to a publisher. Your name and address should be at the top of the page. The approximate length of your manuscript should appear in the right-hand corner. Then skip to about the middle of your page (16-18 lines or so) and type your title in all caps. Type your name underneath your title. Then skip three or four spaces and start your story.

Be certain to double space and use only one side of the paper. Make sure that the margins are wide too.

You don't need to include a page number on the first page of your story.

Your Cover Letter

Like a query letter, a cover letter should entice an editor to read your manuscript, and should do so in a straightforward manner. Because cover letters are read quickly, they must be short and to the point. The editor needs to know what you are sending, who the target reader is, why you are sending it to their particular publishing company at that particular time and a little bit about you—in that order.

The Sunshine Man, page 2

This is what the next page of your manuscript should look like. At the top of the page, maintain your one-inch margin, type the title of the work and the page number. The rest of the manuscript should be consecutively numbered in the same way.

Remember to proofread your final manuscript several times and to ask a friend or colleague to review it one last time. Make any corrections on your typewriter or word processor. Do not make corrections on the manuscript by hand.

Let's consider the example of a cover letter on page 92. First of all, note that the writer has addressed the cover letter to a specific editor. If you know the name of the editor, use it—it is the only way to ensure that your manuscript gets to that editor's desk. *Children's Writer's and Illustrator's Market*, the publisher's guidelines or industry newsletters may indicate specific editors who are reviewing certain kinds of manuscripts. You can also try calling the publisher to find out which editor is appropriate, but you may have a hard time getting an answer with today's automated switchboards and other corporate obstacles. The Children's Book Editor web site tracks the moves of editors in their special "Who's Moving Where?" section. See page 118 for the site's address. If you don't have an editor's name, don't fret—simply address it to "Editor."

Look at the body of the letter. Here the writer introduces the fact that he is enclosing a manuscript (he could also be enclosing a proposal), gives the title of the manuscript and briefly describes its genre. The writer then tells the editor who he expects the audience for his book to be. Next, the writer explains why he is sending it to that particular house at that particular time. He is not only explaining his rationale for his choice, but he is also demonstrating that he has done his research and knows this particular publishing house is looking for a manuscript like his.

SAMPLE OF MANUSCRIPT FORM—CHAPTER BOOK OR NOVEL

Phillip Lawrence
661 Star Avenue
Gracetown, Louisiana XXXXX
111-444-1234

12000 words

THE MYSTERY OF MALLARD SWAMP
By Phillip Lawrence

Next, the writer describes his writing and publishing credentials. If this is your first foray into the field and you've not yet been published, don't despair. There are other kinds of information you can include here to impress an editor. How many manuscripts have you completed? Do you have any firsthand experience with kids? (Are you a teacher, for example?) Do you have firsthand experience with the subject matter? (If you've written a nonfiction book about beekeeping for kids, do you also raise bees?) Have you done any other kind of writing (technical, marketing, public relations, magazine, etc.)? Have you completed any major course work in this area?

If you do have several published writing credits, even if they are in another field, you can list them either in your cover letter or on a separate sheet if they are substantial.

Look at the writer's closing. He's concluded simply and quickly—thanking the editor for her time and asking for the return of his manuscript.

It's tempting, in these days of computerized word processing, to ask the editor to discard the manuscript and to inform you with a simple acceptance or rejection. This may keep the overall cost down, but it also devalues your work. Think about it: You are suggesting that the editor throw out your work. Even if you have

The Mystery of Mallard Swamp, page 1

Chapter One
THE DISCOVERY

This is what chapter one of your chapter book or novel manuscript should look like when you send it off to a publisher. First, create a title page, with the title in all caps and your byline beneath in the center of the page. Your name, address and social security number should be in the upper left corner, and the manuscript word count in the upper right. The rest of your title page should be blank.

Then skip to about one fourth of the way down the second page and type your chapter title in all caps. Then begin typing your story. Include a page number on the first page of first chapter, and on subsequent pages, along with a heading that includes your book's title. Your entire book should be consecutively numbered. Don't begin every new chapter with page 1.

another copy saved on your computer or in a file at home, this implies that you are comfortable with your work being tossed in a trash can. That's not a very positive statement to make about your writing.

One final word on the cover letter—it is a way to introduce yourself to an editor. It is the first impression you make. The editor will quickly skim it, so be sure to proofread it thoroughly. The point is—don't *agonize* over the content and tone of the letter. Many writers don't ever get around to submitting their work because they feel that they can't get that cover letter down just right.

Taking the Next Step

For many writers, the hardest step in seeking publishing isn't preparing the manuscript in the correct form or writing the cover

SAMPLE COVER LETTER

Phillip Lawrence
661 Star Avenue
Gracetown, Louisiana XXXXX

Date

Laura Stephan
Russell Publishing
78 Camden Way
Cooldale, Vermont XXXXX

Dear Ms. Stephan,

I am pleased to enclose *The Mystery of Mallard Marsh*, a chapter book for early readers, for your consideration. The book will delight seven- to ten-year-old readers, especially those who are interested in nature and mysteries.

In *The Mystery of Mallard Marsh*, a young sleuth uncovers a secret about the mallards who migrate through her town every year. Its ecological theme, as well as its child-centered plot line, make it a perfect fit with Russell Publishing's Young Mysteries chapter book series.

I am a second grade teacher in my hometown of Graceville and an avid bird watcher. I have written several nonfiction articles about ducks and mallards for local newspapers and magazines, and I speak to children on the topic at our community's nature preserve.

I have enclosed an SASE for the return of my manuscript should it not fit your needs. Thank you for considering *The Mystery of Mallard Marsh*. I look forward to hearing from you.

Sincerely,

Phillip Lawrence
enclosures: *The Mystery of Mallard Marsh*, reply postcard, SASE

letter. It's actually putting the manuscript in the mail. To those individuals, submitting a manuscript is *asking* for rejection. It is true that submitting a manuscript to a publisher implies that risk, but it is the only way you will ever see your story in print. It's a risk you simply must take if you intend to be a published writer. And, the more you do it, the less scary it will seem.

So take that all-important risk. Prepare your manuscript—and then mail it. Take some time to celebrate afterwards, to savor the fact that you have just taken a very important step.

Take a little time, too, to record when you sent the manuscript out and to whom. Also note when you can expect to hear from the publisher. Most publishers respond in three months, but their response time does vary. Check the most current guidelines from each publisher to be sure.

Then it's time to move on. Some writers actually report feeling a bit let down when they've finished a manuscript. One way to avoid that let down feeling is to keep writing. Brainstorm some fresh ideas. Work on something new. Revise something you had put on hold. While some writers need to take a break after they submit their work, most feel it is important to keep their writing rhythm going while waiting to hear about a manuscript. It's also helpful to keep submitting work to other publishers so that you have as many "irons in the fire" as possible.

How Long Do I Wait?

Some publishers indicate in their guidelines how long they expect to hold a manuscript before making a decision. If you have waited the prescribed amount of time—about three months, unless the publisher has indicated another period of time—you can write to the publisher and politely and professionally ask about the status of your manuscript. (For an example of a letter requesting such a status report, see page 94. You may also enclose a reply card so the publisher finds it convenient to respond.) The operative words here are *politely* and *professionally*. Making demands or forcefully asking about the manuscript will only get it rejected. It's almost always better to write a letter than to fax or call. (Some publishers

SAMPLE LETTER REQUESTING STATUS OF MANUSCRIPT

Douglas Phillips
45 Baltimore Place
Seneca City, West Virginia XXXXX

Kaitlin Christopher
Sherpa Press
774 Long Ridge Drive
Feldspar, Maryland XXXXX

Dear Ms. Christopher,

I am writing about my manuscript, *The Great Golf Ball Adventure*, that I sent to you on July 2. Have you had a chance to review it? Could you let me know on the enclosed postcard when I can expect to hear some news?

Thank you for considering my request—and my manuscript.

Sincerely,

Douglas Phillips

may respond to requests for updates made through e-mail, however.)

Keep in mind that the longer a publisher holds onto a manuscript, the better the news might be. When I was an editor, I quickly rejected the manuscripts that were clearly not appropriate for my publisher. The manuscripts with potential stayed on my desk just a little longer, until I had time to write an encouraging letter or make suggestions for revision.

What Does Rejection Mean?

Since you probably feel emotionally invested in your story, you will likely find rejection a huge disappointment. But don't let it take the wind out of your sails for too long.

Most publishers have a standard form stating they cannot use your manuscript at this particular time. You'll find rejection easier if you recognize that this statement means exactly what it says. It's not a rejection of you or, in most cases, the quality of your writing. It simply means that your manuscript was not right for that particular publisher.

Consider yourself fortunate if you receive a rejection with a handwritten or typewritten note from the editor who read the work. The editor may explain a bit more about why the manuscript didn't work. He may encourage you to make certain revisions and resubmit it. If you receive notes like this, respond to the editors, thanking them for their constructive criticism and informing them if you are planning to resubmit. If you've received some encouragement, make sure you keep your name in front of that editor's eyes as much as possible.

Acceptances and Other Good News

There are few things as wonderful as receiving good news from a publisher—they want to publish your book manuscript! Usually, this kind of news comes by phone rather than through the mail. The editor who will handle the manuscript generally makes the congratulatory call. They may make a few suggestions for revision before discussing contract terms, or they may give you a general idea about the kind of contract you can expect. Then they usually follow up the conversation with a confirming letter.

If you're like most people, you'll be jumping up and down for joy. Most editors expect that kind of reaction. Try to maintain your professional composure as much as you can though, because you'll want to make notes about what the editor tells you. And, while you will most likely accept the contract terms they offer, it's best to give yourself a little "thinking" time before you confirm—even verbally. Most book contracts are fairly standard in terms of what they offer. You'll find more information on contract terms on page 96.

What do you do if you have sent your manuscript to several publishers and have only heard from one? If you are a first-time author, you are probably not in the position to encourage a bidding

Contract Basics

When presented with a contract, most of us feel the urge to rush to our attorney's office and have it reviewed. While it's probably the right reaction for most contracts, unless your attorney knows the logistics of literary contracts, it is probably not your best move.

Here are some general terms you will find in your contract:

- A description of your manuscript, including the length.
- The due date for the manuscript or for any revisions.
- The amount you will be paid. Generally, you will be paid either a flat fee or an advance upon signing the contract and/or completing an acceptable manuscript. You may also receive a royalty or percentage of sales. Standard royalties range from 7-12 percent of *net* profits. Remember that you do not begin receiving royalties until you have "earned back" any advances.
- An explanation of what your "rights" to the manuscript are. (This will include how much of a percentage you might receive for film rights or electronic media, for example.)
- An indication of who retains copyright. (It's always best to hold the copyright in your name rather than the publisher's.)
- A clause stating the number of free copies you receive of your book, any discounts under which you may purchase additional books and the terms under which you can resell them.
- An option clause, stating that the publisher has the right to review your next work for publication.

For most publishers, the last three terms are generally negotiable. The amount of advance and royalty may be negotiable within a range, but is fairly standard.

war among publishers. Instead, it's wisest to inform the other publishers that you are withdrawing your manuscript from consideration. There's no need to explain the situation any further.

It's Your Story

There are hundreds of books written and seminars given about how to approach publishers and book editors with a book manuscript. While there's no mystery or magic about the process, there is also no way of knowing what will strike an editor's fancy at any particular time.

To Agent or Not to Agent

Do you need an agent to sell your manuscript to a publisher? In children's book publishing, having an agent is not essential to getting printed. If you are an unpublished author, you may find it difficult to get an agent in any case. Many agents simply don't take on clients who don't have an established track record.

There are agents, though, who accept unpublished authors, especially if your manuscript fits nicely with the other material they represent. There are a number of advantages to seeking an agent.

- Agents generally have an inside track on who's publishing what. They know the editors and how to approach them.
- Agents can usually strike better financial deals and can make certain other provisions.
- Agents remove any emotional complications you may have with your editor. (Your editor often becomes a colleague if not a friend, and it's infinitely easier if you don't have to negotiate with a friend.)

But beginning writers need to beware. While most agents are ethical and scrupulous people, there are some who take advantage of an author's burning desire to be published.

If you have an agent, keep in mind the following suggestions:

- Meet your agent face to face. If at all possible, meet in her office. This may mean a trip to New York, but it is the best way to determine if she is legitimate.
- If she charges a reading fee, make sure it is within the range you are willing to pay.
- Confirm that she is a member of the Association of Author's Representatives.
- In your agreement, stipulate that you have access to the publisher.
- She must provide you with a list of submissions and proof that she actually did submit the manuscripts.
- Keep yourself informed of her submissions and make sure she submits to the appropriate publishers.
- Confirm your negotiating guidelines with her.
- Agree on how you will work on revisions.
- Decide before entering a relationship with an agent if you are willing to let her take a cut (10-15 percent if she is representing just the manuscript, higher if she represents the art, too). ✸

Ultimately, it's the strength of your story that is going to attract an editor. Choosing appropriate publishers, preparing your manuscript professionally and submitting it with a professional cover letter will make an editor take your work seriously, but it's the work itself that makes the impression.

It's important to know these general guidelines, but it's more important to work at the *craft* of writing. Submit appropriately—but submit work you have worked hard at and are proud of. Believe in yourself as a writer and submit work you believe in. That's where the real magic happens.

Tips From the Top

1. Never fax manuscripts, proposals or query letters for book manuscripts. (Although this is acceptable for some magazines and other periodicals, it is not accepted in the book world.)

2. Submit clean manuscripts. Do not send out a manuscript that is dog-eared or looks as if it has been read by several other editors. Print out a new copy.

3. Use a standard typeface like Courier, Helvetica or New York. Don't use many different fonts or a fancy cursive font.

4. Make sure your manuscript is easy to read. Replace old ribbons or printer cartridges before printing the final copy.

5. Ask for the return of your manuscript. Do not suggest to the publisher that they can throw it away.

6. Be direct in your cover and query letters. Impress upon the editor that you have done your research and explain why your manuscript is appropriate for their particular publishing company.

7. Proofread your letters carefully. A letter full of errors will immediately give the wrong impression—and may stop an editor from reading your story entirely. Check the body carefully, but also check your name, the editor's name, the publishing company, etc. If you are writing a standard letter and sending it to a few different publishers, make sure you change the particulars—the editor's name, the publishing company, the date, etc.

8. Make sure your return envelope is the appropriate size and has the appropriate postage.

9. Submit your work appropriately—and often. The more manuscripts you submit, the stronger the likelihood that you will achieve publishing success.

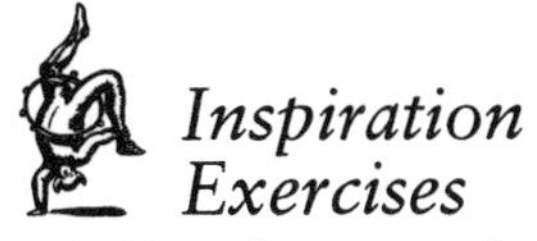

Inspiration Exercises

1. Practice summing up one of your story's themes in a single sentence. Start with, "This story is about . . . " and try to capture the essence of the story in the rest of the sentence. You may want to include a version of this sentence in your cover letter to describe the piece you are submitting.

2. List the various experiences you have had in relation to the book you have written. Now pick a couple of them to include in the author statement in your cover letter.

3. Practice writing cover and query letters by pretending to be a published author pitching a classic work. (Write a cover letter in which Mark Twain describes *The Adventures of Huckleberry Finn*, for instance, or Judy Blume tries to sell *Superfudge*.)

4. Practice writing cover letters and query letters for an existing work or for one you plan to write.

8 BREAKING INTO PRINT

Here's an inside tip that sounds simple and impossible at the same time: Write as much as you can, publish as often as possible. If you can be creative both about the way you write and the way you look for publishing opportunities, you *can* make this formula work for you.

Finding Your Writing Rhythm

First of all, consider the first part of that formula: Write as much as you can. The most common complaint I hear from people who want to write children's books is that they can't find the time to actually write. Often, a lack of time is not the problem. It's the fact that the would-be writer hasn't yet discovered her personal "writing rhythm."

It's not only important to find the time to write, it's important to find the *right* time to write. We all have times of the day and times of the year when we are more productive and creative. I find that I am most creative in the morning, so that's when I do the majority of my writing. I get up before the rest of my family and steal a couple of hours at dawn. Of course, like most people, I would prefer to sleep in, but I force myself to get up because I know this is my best time of day. By noon, I usually quit and, unless I have a pressing deadline, I don't return to my writing until the next day.

It's also important to set realistic goals for yourself. Some writers commit to writing for a certain period of time every day. Others—and I'm in this group—set a goal of how many pages to produce. Either method will work: Just make sure your goal is attainable so you don't feel as if you are consistently falling short.

It may also help to develop a writing method such as the one I call "writing on the fly." I usually don't have large blocks of time—like a couple of hours—to write, so I've learned not to need them. Instead, I manage to steal ten or fifteen minutes here and there throughout the day. Even if I only get a few sentences down, I feel as if I am moving forward.

I also am able to write just about anywhere. I frequently take my laptop along with me and work during my kids' soccer practices. I always have a paper and pencil ready as well. I am prepared to take advantage of *any* time that is available, even if that time is unexpected.

Finally, I have learned to shut out external noise and activity. I have learned not to need absolute silence in order to focus on the task at hand. Instead, I am able to work even in the midst of my own kids' ruckus.

If you feel you need absolute quiet or substantial blocks of time in order to write, I urge you to try and develop some of these "writing on the fly" techniques. Writing with kids yelling in the background or in the car waiting for school to let out isn't easy—and it certainly wasn't easy for me at first. While these conditions aren't optimal, if you do it often enough, you'll probably develop a way to make it work. I find writing at these frenzied times *and* during my morning hours gives me a good balance and increases my productivity.

Be careful of the writer's block trap. You probably feel more creative on some days than others, but don't let that stop you from writing. Sit down and get something—anything—on paper. Even if the writing's not wonderful, at least you will have something to revise.

Considering All Publishing Opportunities

Now let's look at the second half of that formula: Publish as much as possible. The best way to accomplish this is by looking for

Finding Your Creative Style

Every writer has his or her creative style. One writer may prefer to write in the middle of the night, while another is more creative at the crack of dawn. One writer may need his writing space neat and uncluttered, with only his current project on his desk, while another feels more comfortable with piles of paper, objects of inspiration and lots of resource guides piled high on his table. One writer prefers the computer, while another writes by hand.

You can make some assumptions about your writing style by looking at the ways you are productive in other areas. Consider these questions about your writing schedule and writing space:

- **Are you a morning person or a night person?** If you pop right out of bed in the morning ready to face your day, you are probably most creative in the morning hours and you'll want to schedule writing time then. If you wake slowly and tend to be a night owl, you may want to save time in the evening or late at night to devote to writing. Don't make assumptions based on what you *think* you are. Experiment with different time slots. As you do, make sure you note how you feel about the work you are doing. After a week or so, go back and review the writing you did. Do you feel the same way about it as you did when you wrote it?
- **Can you sit still for a long period of time?** If you are able to sit still without interrupting yourself—getting a snack, flipping on the television, talking on the phone—you will probably be able to schedule a longer writing time for each sitting. If, on the other hand, you are constantly moving around, you may want to schedule shorter, more frequent writing intervals. To determine which style suits you, sit for an hour at your computer and write. Record how many times you actually wanted to get up and move around. Then decide which writing rhythm suits you best.
- **Do you frequently lose or misplace material?** If so, you may want to write on the computer and make copies of your work, both on paper and on disk. While making copies causes clutter, at least you won't permanently lose a masterpiece.
- **Do you write quickly and revise extensively? Or do you ponder every word before you write it down?** Think about how much time you actually devote to the physical act of writing. If you make very sloppy and rough first drafts, using writing as part of the actual

creative process, you need to build in a great deal of revision time before the due date. If you think first, then write, your first draft will probably be closer to the final. Your manuscript may not need as much revision.

- **Do you need lots of social interaction?** If you are a real "people person" with lots of friendships and relationships, you may find that you need to be more deliberate about scheduling meetings with friends. Otherwise, you might fritter away valuable time that is necessary for solitary writing and thinking. Likewise, if you are comfortable being alone with only your words for comfort, you'll need to consider scheduling social time so you don't lose objectivity about your work or valuable relationships with friends and colleagues.

creative publishing opportunities. Most writers know about traditional publishing houses—the ones that publish mainstream books for the bookstore market. There are many other categories of publishers though, and several offer *real* opportunities to beginning writers. While these opportunities may not be as lucrative or as high profile as publishing with a traditional publishing house, they can be a way to get your work into print, and they can help you add publishing credits to your credentials.

Packaging Companies

A packaging company (sometimes called a development house or book producer) is a kind of publishing company that produces books for traditional publishing houses. Most packagers work in this way: They conceive an idea for a book or book series and then propose the idea to a publishing company. If the publishing company likes the idea, they buy the book or book series in its conceptual form. The packaging company then hires the writers and the artists. The packager edits and designs the book, with the publishing company having approval rights. In some cases, the packager typesets the manuscript and even sends it to the printer.

To find out more about packaging companies, write for their guidelines. They may be seeking writers who have fresh ideas, or they might need writers for specific series that they already have in the works. Sometimes, packagers even let writers "try out" by writing a sample chapter based on a plot outline they provide.

There are a couple of things you should know before you work with a packager. Due to the arrangement, you often will be writing under someone else's name and will probably not be able to retain the copyright in your name. You will probably be paid a flat fee with no royalties, and you may also be asked to turn work around extremely quickly.

When writing for a packager, the biggest consideration you need to make is your ability and willingness to write to someone else's formula. Many writers find this very restricting. Others learn a lot about their own writing and the publishing industry from the experience. You'll find book packagers listed in *Literary Marketplace* and *Children's Writer's and Illustrator's Market.*

Educational Publishers

Educational publishers hire writers for projects other than textbooks. They look for individuals who can produce nonfiction and fiction books, as well as workbooks for use in the classroom or home-school settings. Educational publishers have a need for creative and imaginative picture books that allow teachers to apply whole language or phonics principles. They are also looking for writers who can produce material that meets specific state curricula or proficiency testing requirements.

If you have teaching experience or a teaching degree, you'll have a definite advantage with an educational publisher. If not, you can get a leg up on this market by learning about the teaching methods and subjects at various grade levels. You can gain this information by requesting the curriculum from your state board of education or by visiting classrooms, talking to teachers and volunteering in schools.

Again, start by writing for guidelines. You can find educational publishers in *Children's Writer's and Illustrator's Market*, *Literary Marketplace* and in Sandra Warren's *How to Publish Those "Great" Classroom Ideas.* Packaging companies often produce material for educational publishers too.

SAMPLE LETTER REQUESTING GUIDELINES FROM A PACKAGER

Beth Sanders
44 Lavender Lane
Jennydale, Utah XXXXX

Date

Paul Pippin
Duncan Packaging Group
440 Donner Road
Chicago, IL XXXXX

Dear Mr. Pippin,

I am a writer of juvenile nonfiction and am interested in learning about writing opportunities with your book-packaging firm. Please send me your general guidelines, as well as specific guidelines for any nonfiction book series you might be developing. I have enclosed an SASE for your convenience.

Sincerely,

Beth Sanders

Religious Publishers

Religious publishers look for writers who can create books that reflect their specific spiritual beliefs or scriptural interpretations. Religious publishers are more specialized than larger publishing houses. For instance, Christian publishers might focus on producing books with strong religious themes or books that are more general in nature but reflect Christian principles. There are also publishers that publish for specific niches of the Christian market—texts for Sunday school and Bible school, youth ministries and leaders, Christian schools and home-schoolers, and so on. For additional information about Christian publishers, consult the *Christian Writers' Market Guide.*

Although Christian publishers are the largest segment of this market, there are publishers with interest in other religions as well. Two examples are the Jewish Publication Society and the B'Hai Publishing Trust. Write for the publishers' guidelines to find out each publisher's specific needs.

Magazines

There are many more opportunities to be published in children's magazines than in children's books. Magazines need writers of fiction, nonfiction and feature stories. You can find out about children's magazines in *Children's Writer's and Illustrator's Market* and then write for guidelines. Be sure to spend some time studying the magazines to get a flavor for the writing style, reading level and approach of each one. You can request sample issues from the publisher or look for them at your local library.

Publishing in children's magazines can help you break into book publishing in a couple of important ways. The magazine credits will give you credibility with a book publisher. You can "try out" an idea for a book in magazine form. Some book editors even read children's magazines looking for appropriate authors for specific projects.

Book Fairs and Book Clubs

Book fairs are fundraising programs for schools in which a company brings books to the school for kids to purchase. The school receives part of the sale profits or is awarded free books or other premiums. A book club works in a similar way, except the students order the books from a form that is sent home from school.

Book fairs and clubs generally resell books that they purchase from other publishers, in addition to books they publish themselves. These publishers usually specialize in paperback books with immediate kid appeal since the young readers are generally making their own purchase decisions. Again, writing for guidelines is the best way to learn more about these publishers' needs. Keep in mind that most book fair companies offer limited bookstore exposure. While your books will be getting into the hands of lots of young readers, they will be getting there through a school setting rather than a traditional bookstore.

Vanity Presses and Self-Publishing

If you've been rejected a number of times, you may turn to a vanity press—a press that requires *you* to pay for part or all of the publication of your book. Many vanity presses promise much more than they can deliver, everything from marketing expertise to national distribution and a publicity effort.

A better alternative is self-publishing—directly handling the publication of the book yourself. While you are responsible for all of the costs of publication, you have control over all of the elements of the book. You also receive all of the profits, not just a percentage. If the book is produced well and sells fairly well, a publisher might actually pick it up and publish it under its own name.

Today's technology makes self-publishing seem deceptively easy. Most people think all it really takes to prepare a manuscript for publication is some basic knowledge of word processing and design software. Although technology has made things easier, you'll need to acquire some knowledge of book design, typesetting, printing, binding, distribution and marketing if you want the book to compete on the bookstore shelves. And if your book is illustrated, you'll need to learn a good deal about art reproduction as well.

In most communities, there are consultants or companies who can offer advice on how all this gets done. Many printing companies will offer free advice to writers who are using their printing services. Unless you intend your book to be for a small audience—your own children or grandchildren, for instance—you would be wise to seek professional help.

Don't neglect the important steps of editing and proofreading if you are self-publishing. Again, these are best done by someone other than yourself, someone who will bring an objective eye to the project.

Finally, be prepared to be writer-editor-publisher *and* publicist and sales representative all wrapped up into one. It will be up to you to make sure your book gets into the hands of book reviewers and onto the bookstores' shelves. You should be aware that many newspapers and review media don't review self-published books or books published by vanity presses. It is also difficult to achieve national distribution for a self-published book. You'll need to promote your book with signings, seminars and public appearances. Individual consultants can help you handle this part of the process too, but you'll probably end up organizing a large part of it yourself.

Treating Yourself as a Professional

When I first quit my "day job" to write full time, I had trouble explaining what I did for a living. Even though I had already been published, I couldn't say the important words that defined my career—I am a writer. It was only when I began to define myself in those terms that I began to feel good about my writing and was able to produce my best work.

I also learned the importance of treating my writing career with the same commitment as the "real job" I had left. For example, I seemed to produce better and more consistent work if I dressed every day just as I had for the office. I had a separate phone line installed just for my fax machine and my writing calls. I had business cards made and opened a separate bank account for any proceeds from book sales. I learned to ignore those constant distractions—the phone, the television, the refrigerator. In short, writing became my job.

If you're like most people, you're not going to give up your day job to write children's books, but you can still begin to treat yourself as a professional. Defining yourself as a writer is the first—and most important—step. If you want to be a writer, start *calling* yourself a writer.

Say the words with conviction and pride.

If It Sounds Too Good to Be True, It Probably Is

Traditional publishing is, for the most part, an ethical business. However, there are companies, contests and other programs that take advantage of writers who are desperate to see their name in print. Be wary of the following pitches:

- Contests that require a large entry fee, more than $25 or so.
- Contests that promise publication only. The only "reward" you may receive is the opportunity to purchase the book in which your poem, short story or nonfiction piece is printed. Your piece of writing will usually appear printed with the work of hundreds of other eager writers just like you. The book itself will probably not be distributed to anyone but the people who have a piece in it.
- Vanity presses that promise your book will receive wide national recognition or be promoted through a slickly designed catalog. Most vanity presses do a very poor job of getting their books to the general public. You are paying for the entire publication of the book, after all. They have no real stake in how many copies are sold.
- Magazines that pay their writers in free copies. While many literary magazines engage in this practice as a matter of course, most magazines aimed at children pay *something* to their writers, even if it is a small amount. They should provide several free copies to you as a matter of course.

This is not to say that these opportunities aren't worth pursuing, especially if you have a burning desire to see your name in print. Just be clear about what you are getting yourself into. Don't expect more than the publisher can deliver. And remember the old saying—if it sounds too good to be true, it probably is. ✵

Don't fall prey to those negative *buts* or *somedays*. Say "I am a writer," instead of "I want to be a writer someday." And say it often.

Remember, too, that you aren't just any writer. You write for the most special people in the world—children. You are a writer and you are shaping our future. You are a writer and you are enriching and inspiring young minds. You are a writer and you are educating and informing young readers.

You are a writer and you write for children.

Now, go write!

Giving Something Back

Since you've chosen to write for children, you no doubt already care deeply about kids and their well-being. You may then find it rewarding to act on your conviction not only by writing, but by working directly with, or for, children. You'll not only enhance their lives, but you will have experiences that will enrich your own writing.

Consider these opportunities that relate directly to writing and reading:

- Volunteer for a literacy organization. This may involve volunteering at fund-raising functions or actually working as a tutor with a child or adult who is having difficulty reading.
- Volunteer at schools, by reading to kids, shelving books in the school library, or coordinating their book fairs or reading programs. It's a great way to learn about books and publishers.
- Mentor a young writer.
- If you are qualified, volunteer to conduct writing workshops for kids at community centers, day camps or other places where kids gather.
- Explore "friends groups" and other volunteer opportunities at libraries and literary centers.
- Find time to read to a child in need—at a homeless shelter, hospital, children's home, etc. ✵

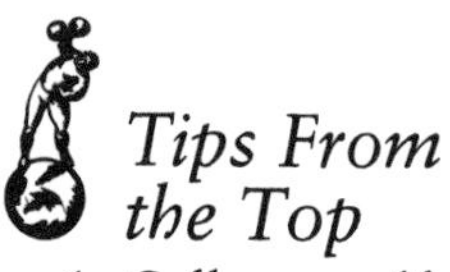

Tips From the Top

1. Call yourself a writer. Instead of saying "I do freelance writing" or "I write," say "I am a writer."

2. Be creative about finding publishing opportunities. Investigate writing opportunities in your own backyard. Are there parenting newspapers, local newspapers, trade magazines or other publications in your community? Find out what there are and how they hire their writers.

3. Set specific writing goals. Goals may include amount of time spent writing, number of pages produced, number of manuscripts completed or number of manuscripts submitted.

4. Set up a writing schedule that works for you. Don't put off writing because you can't find a block of uninterrupted time. Instead, make time. Master the art of writing on the fly. Get up a couple of hours earlier in the morning.

5. Submit your manuscripts! Take that all-important step of sending your manuscripts out!

6. Take some time to think about your role as a writer in the world. Look for volunteer opportunities that are consistent with your mission as a writer.

7. Treat yourself as a professional. Make sure your manuscript looks professional. Attack your writing with professional enthusiasm. Deal with publishers and editors with a professional attitude.

Inspiration Exercises

1. Make yourself sit and write for thirty minutes straight. Don't move from your seat at all. If you feel blocked or stuck, force yourself to brainstorm or doodle. The next day, increase the amount of time to forty-five minutes. When you are comfortable, try an entire hour of writing. See if you can continue this hour-long writing habit for five days. If you find you are producing work you might refine and finish, continue this habit.

2. Make a writing contract with yourself or with another writing friend. Agree to write for a certain amount of time or to produce a certain number of pages. Come up with a way to reward yourself if you maintain your habit for a month.

3. With a friend or to yourself, commit to submitting a manuscript to a publisher at regular intervals—the third Tuesday of every other month, for instance. Make a date to go to the post office with that friend and mail off the manuscript. Then find a way to celebrate this important step.

4. Research writing conferences and workshops in your area. You may find information on bulletin boards in libraries and literary centers. You may also find such events listed in literary sections of a metropolitan newspaper. Find a workshop that fits your lifestyle, schedule, writing goals and finances, and commit to attend.

5. Read a book by an expert on how he or she goes about the writing process. (You'll find a list of such books in the appendix.) See if you can apply any of their advice to your own life and writing habits. Start making a list of writing tips that experts offer both in books and in seminars or conferences you attend.

6. Visit your library and read at least one newsletter or publishing-related magazine a week.

7. Study the last three issues of three popular children's magazines. Think of three topics for articles or stories that you could write to submit to the magazines that you've selected. Then, if you are excited about pursuing the magazine market, write for the guidelines.

8. Read a number of books from the major religious publishing houses, including a couple of series titles. Think about whether this market is one that you might like to pursue. If it is, write to request guidelines.

9. Create an inviting writing place for yourself. Even if your work space is only the corner of your kitchen table, think about including something in it that is inspirational and inviting.

APPENDIX

Recommended Reading

Books About Writing for Children

1996 Children's Book Market: The Writer's Sourcebook, editor, Institute of Children's Literature.

Children's Writer's and Illustrator's Market: 850 Places to Sell Your Writing and Illustrations, Alice Pope, editor, Writer's Digest Books.

The Christian Writers' Market Guide, Sally Stuart, editor, Harold Shaw Publishing.

Gates of Excellence: On Reading and Writing Books for Children, Katherine Paterson, Dutton.

How to Get Your Teaching Ideas Published: A Writer's Guide to Educational Publishing, Jean Stangl, Walker Books.

How to Publish Those "Great" Classroom Ideas, Sandra Warren, Creative Learning Consultants.

How to Write a Children's Book and Get It Published, Barbara Seuling, Scribners.

How to Write and Illustrate Children's Books and Get Them Published, edited by Treld Pelkey Bicknell and Felicity Trotman, North Light Books.

How to Write and Sell Children's Picture Books, Jean E. Karl, Writer's Digest Books.

The Seed and the Vision: On the Writing and Appreciation of Children's Books, Eleanor Cameron, Dutton Children's Books.

Ten Steps to Publishing Children's Books, Berthe Amoss and Eric Suben, Writer's Digest Books.

The Way to Write for Children, Joan Aiken, St. Martin's Press.

Worlds of Childhood: The Art and Craft of Writing for Children, Jean Fritz et al., edited by William Zinsser, Houghton Mifflin.

Writing and Illustrating Children's Books for Publication, Berthe Amoss and Eric Suben, Writer's Digest Books.

Writing and Publishing Books for Children in the 1990s: The Inside Story From the Editor's Desk, Olga Litowinsky, Walker and Company.

Writing Books for Children, Jane Yolen, The Writer.

Writing Books for Young People, James E. Giblin, The Writer.

Writing for Children, Catherine Woolley, New American Library.

Writing for Children and Teenagers, Lee Wyndham and Arnold Madison, Writer's Digest Books.

Books About Writing in General

The 38 Most Common Fiction Writing Mistakes, Jack M. Bickham, Writer's Digest Books.

The Author's Handbook, Franklynn Peterson and Judi Kesselman-Turkel, Prentice-Hall.

Creating Characters: How to Build Story People, Dwight V. Swain, Writer's Digest Books.

The Fiction Dictionary, Laurie Henry, Story Press.

Fiction Writer's Workshop, Josip Novakovich, Story Press.

Guide to Literary Agents, Donya Dickerson, editor, Writer's Digest Books.

How to Write a Book Proposal, Michael Larsen, Writer's Digest Books.

How to Write Plots That Sell, F.A. Rockwell, Contemporary Books.

The Insider's Guide to Book Editors and Publishers, Jeff Herman, Prima Publishing.

The Insider's Guide to Literary Agents, Jeff Herman, Prima Publishing.

Knowing Where to Look: The Ultimate Guide to Research, Lois Horowitz, Writer's Digest Books.

The Writer's Legal Guide, Tad Crawford and Tony Lyons, Writer's Digest Books.

The Writer's Survival Guide, Rachel Simon, Story Press.

The Writer's Ultimate Research Guide, Ellen Metter, Writer's Digest Books.

Books About Writing and Creativity

Bird by Bird: Some Instructions on Writing and Life, Anne Lamott, Doubleday.
The Crosswicks Journal, Books 1-3, Madeleine L'Engle, Harper.
The Courage to Write: How Writers Transcend Fear, Ralph Keyes, Henry Holt.
Drawing on the Right Side of the Brain: A Course in Enhancing Creativity and Artistic Confidence, Betty Edwards, J.P. Tarcher Books.
Walking on Alligators: A Book of Meditations for Writers, Susan Shaughnessy, Harper San Francisco.
Writing Down the Bones: Freeing the Writer Within, Natalie Goldberg, Shambhala Press.

Books About Style, Grammar and Other Technical Matters

Chicago Manual of Style, John Grossman, managing editor, University of Chicago Press.
Children's Writer's Word Book, Alijandra Mogilner, Writer's Digest Books.
The Elements of Style, William Strunk, Jr. and E.B. White, MacMillan.
Grammatically Correct: The Writer's Guide to Punctuation, Spelling, Style, Usage and Grammar, Anne Stilman, Writer's Digest Books.
The Writer's Essential Desk Reference, Second Edition, the editors of Writer's Digest Books, Writer's Digest Books.

Other Helpful Resources

American Children's Folklore, Simon J. Bronner, August House Publishing.
Don't Tell the Grown-Ups: Why Kids Love the Books They Do, Alison Lurie, Avon.

Organizations

Authors League of America, Inc.
330 West 42 Street, New York, NY 10036

This organization is primarily an advocacy group which sponsors and initiates legislation protecting authors from unfair taxes and other financial entrapments, and it promotes the author's interest in copyright and free speech issues.

PEN American Center
568 Broadway, New York, NY 10012

This international group promotes a national community of writers and is involved in advocating their rights and freedoms.

Romance Writers of America
13700 Veterans Memorial Dr., Suite 315, Houston, TX 77014

The primary organization for those writing in the romance category, Romance Writers of America also has a special organization devoted entirely to young adult literature. The organization sponsors contests, provides market advice and offers regional and national conferences.

Society of Children's Book Writers and Illustrators (SCBWI)
345 N. Maple Dr., Suite 296, Beverly Hills, CA 90210

The largest organization of children's book writers and illustrators in the country, the SCBWI is a professional guild that serves as a "consolidated voice for professional writers and illustrators across the nation." The organization offers an excellent newsletter, regional conferences, financial grants and other benefits, such as health insurance and access to a credit union. The SCBWI also sponsors a free manuscript/illustration exchange and a grant assistance program for works in progress.

Newsletters

Children's Book Insider
P.O. Box 1030, Fairplay, CO 80440-1030

This newsletter features market information, but is primarily devoted to articles on the craft of writing books for children.

Children's Writer
The Institute of Children's Literature
93 Long Ridge Road, West Redding, CT 06896
This newsletter contains market information and articles on the craft of writing, as well as information about contests.

SCBWI Bulletin
Society of Children's Book Writers and Illustrators
22736 Vanowen, Suite 106, West Hills, CA 91307
This bimonthly newsletter contains market tips, information on the publishing activities of its members, interviews with editors, and news on regional meetings and other offerings.

Correspondence Schools

The Institute of Children's Literature
93 Long Ridge Rd., West Redding, CT 06896
Toll-free 1-800-243-9645
This correspondence school offers excellent instructional materials that guide the writer in writing and seeking publication. Published children's authors act as instructors, providing one-on-one instruction and mentoring.

Resources on the Internet

Aaron's Kidwriter Page
http://www.aaronshep.com/kidwriter/index.html
Aaron Shepherd maintains this web site which includes articles on the "nuts and bolts" of writing for children, practical advice, and lists of resources (both online and print).

The Children's Book Council
http://www.cbcbooks.org
This web site includes the membership list of the Children's Book Council, which is updated monthly. While it does not include every children's book publisher, it does list every one that is a member of the council, with names, addresses, phone numbers, names and titles of editors, and a description of the publishing program.

A Children's Book Editor's Site
http://www.users.interport.net/~hdu

At this site, you'll find a growing list of articles that cover the full range of children's writing and illustrating, including submission, interviews, craft, and so on. A Who's Moving Where? section tracks personnel moves at children's book publishers, helping to answer that all-important question—How can I find the right editor's name?

The Children's Writing Resource Center
http://www.write4kids.com/index.html

The Children's Book Insider maintains this site which features articles that originally appeared in their newsletter, a children's writer's message board and chat room, a research center with a list of links to research sites, and subscription information about *CBI*.

Inkspot
http://www.inkspot.com

This site offers outstanding features for writers of all genres. Specific material for children's writers includes a Children's Author Directory (a list of children's authors who maintain web sites) and a list of internet sites with links for newsletters, books and organizations that are helpful for children's writers. This site also features a free biweekly e-mail newsletter which includes articles and marketing tips, many of them relevant to children's authors.

The Society of Children's Book Writers and Illustrators
http://www.scbwi.org

The web site of the SCBWI details membership benefits, requirements and procedures for grants, information about writing conferences throughout the country, and articles on the craft of writing. The web site also includes an SCBWI membership application.

INDEX